THE AGE OF MISSING INFORMATION

The Age of

MISSING INFORMATION

Bill McKIBBEN

RANDOM HOUSE TRADE PAPERBACKS
NEW YORK

2006 Random House Trade Paperback Edition

Published in the United States by Random House Trade Paperbacks, an imprint of The Random House Publishing Group, a division of Random House, Inc., New York.

RANDOM HOUSE TRADE PAPERBACKS and colophon are trademarks of Random House, Inc.

Portions of this work originally appeared in *The New Yorker* as "Reflections: What's On?"

Originally published in hardcover in the United States by Random House, an imprint of The Random House Publishing Group, a division of Random House, Inc., in 1992. Published in paperback by Plume, an imprint of Dutton Signet, a division of Penguin Books USA, in 1993.

Grateful acknowledgment is made to the following for permission to reprint previously published material:

NOEL RIEDINGER-JOHNSON: Seven lines from a poem by Jeanne Robert Foster from *Adirondack Portraits: A Piece of Time*, edited by Noel Riedinger-Johnson, copyright © 1986 by Noel Riedinger-Johnson. Reprinted by permission.

VARRY WHITE MUSIC, INC.: Excerpt from "Bust a Move" written by M. Young, Matt Kike, and Michael Ross, copyright © 1989 by Varry White Music, Inc. Reprinted by permission.

BMG MUSIC PUBLISHING, INC., AND BMG MUSIC PUBLISHING CANADA: Excerpt from "Pump That Body" by Robert Smith/Lee Haggard, copyright © 1990 by Zomba Enterprises, Inc. (ASCAP)/House Jam Music (ASCAP). All rights in the U.S. on behalf of House Jam Music (ASCAP) are administered by Zomba Enterprises (ASCAP). Rights outside the U.S. are administered by BMG Music Publishing Canada. All rights reserved. Used by permission.

LIBRARY OF CONGRESS CATALOGING-IN-PUBLICATION DATA

McKibben, Bill.

The age of missing information / Bill McKibben.

p. cm.

Includes index.

ISBN 0-8129-7607-X

1. Television broadcasting—Social aspects—United States. 2. United States—Popular culture. 3. Nature. 4. Philosophy of nature. I. Title.

PN1992.6. M38 1992b 302.23'45'0973—dc20 92-40397

Printed in the United States of America

www.atrandom.com

2 4 6 8 9 7 5 3

For my parents,
Gordon and Peggy McKibben

ACKNOWLEDGMENTS

Most acknowledgments end by thanking one's spouse. I want to reverse the traditional order in this case—Sue was as always a marvelous editor, but she also made this project possible simply by putting up with it. I spent eight-hour days for many months watching cartoons and soap operas and shopping channels and televangelists, with predictable mood-altering effect. For her good humor she has my gratitude, and my promise I'll never do anything quite so daft again.

I obviously owe a great debt of thanks to the many people in Fairfax who helped me collect the videotape that made this project possible. Many of these volunteers were organized by Channel 10, a local community access station that is a model for similar operations around the country. I would also like to thank Janet Dueweke, Richard Rubenstein, Michael and Shawn Leary Considine, Erin Leary Wence, and David Roe.

The trails on Crow Mountain, the Adirondack peak described at length in this book, are maintained by Steve Ovitt, an exceptionally able New York State forest ranger. (By the way, Crow is not its real name.) Noel Riedinger-Johnson helped me see the mountain through the eyes of poet and native daughter Jeanne Robert Foster. I'd also like to thank the people of Johnsburg Methodist Church, who have helped me especially to understand the meaning of community.

I have found the work of many writers helpful as I've considered the themes of this book. Mark Crispin Miller, David Marc, Jerry Mander, Ron Powers, Todd Gitlin, Neil Postman, Tom Shales, Walter Goodman, and a great many others have written incisively about television; George Trow, a dear friend and colleague, has made me think very hard about the media, and I am immensely grateful to him. As I was working on this project, a friend, Jim Gustafson of Emory University, sent me two books that I found both congenial and illuminating—Albert Borgmann's *Technology and the Character of Contemporary Life* and Erazim Kohak's lovely *The Embers and the Stars.* And, as always, my debt to the writings of Wendell Berry is profound.

A number of friends have read this manuscript and offered helpful advice, including David Edelstein, Scott Rosenberg, Jeff Toobin, Bill Finnegan, Cynthia Zarin, and Sam and Lisa Verhovek. My agent, Gloria Loomis, helped shape the manuscript right from the start. So, of course, did my editor, David Rosenthal—his assistance has been both good-natured and wise. I would also like to thank their assistants, Kendra Taylor and Rebecca Beuchler. At *The New Yorker*, both John Bennet and Robert Gottlieb gave good counsel, and Hal Espen did his usual fine job of checking the facts. Eleanor Gould Packard, America's premier grammarian, did her usual magnificent job of making clear what I actually meant to say.

Many thanks, finally, to my parents, to whom this book is dedicated. Far more than television they influenced the shape of my life.

THE AGE OF MISSING INFORMATION

7:00 A.M.

If you have a cold, you do not need to worry about reinfecting yourself with your lip balm." That's Beverly, who leads Christian calisthenics on Channel 116, Family Net. "If you used someone else's lip balm, I could see that. But not your own." *So much happens* between seven and eight in the morning on the ninety-three stations of the Fairfax, Virginia, cable system, until recently the largest in the world. On *Good Morning America,* Joel, the movie critic, says, "I learned something about England. For sore throats, the actors of Shakespeare's time used to take a live frog and lower the frog by its foot into their mouths. They figured that would keep the juices going. That's where the expression 'a frog in your throat' comes from." Since seaweed grows "in the nutrient-rich ocean," it comes as no surprise to anyone in the Annushka cosmetics organization that it attacks and destroys cellulite. An Amtrak train has gone off the rails in Iowa, according to CNN, and American companies will now be allowed to sell laptop computers in Eastern Europe. Kevin Johnson of the Phoenix Suns, so racked with the flu he had to be fed intravenously, nonetheless tallied 29 points and 12 assists in last night's game. Meanwhile, a robot surgeon has successfully replaced a dog's arthritic hip with an artificial joint. On the Fox affiliate, a cartoon Mr. Wilson is *sure* that's Dennis (the Menace) in the gorilla suit, so he uses a pair of pliers on the snout; entertainingly, however, it's an actual gorilla escaped from the zoo. The Infiniti Q-45 goes 0–60 in 6.9 seconds—" 'Wow' is an involuntary response of pure pleasure." Type A personalities are five times as likely to have a *second* heart attack, according to Otto Wahl, the psychiatry professor at George Mason University. Following vertical roasting on the Spanik Vertical Roaster, a chicken can be—is—carved with a carrot. In Czechoslovakia, Ambassador Rita Klimova tells C-SPAN, the newly emerging democracy has spawned dozens of political parties, including one for beer drinkers. Sesame Street is brought to you this morning by L, S, and 6. Only 11 percent of Americans feel the penny should be banned. Mr. Wizard is ripping apart fireworks to get at the chemicals inside. "Finally one of my favorites—strontium chloride," he exults. In Japan an exchange has opened to trade memberships in golf clubs as if they were stocks—they are already accepted as collateral by banks. Margie Grant now uses Dove soap: "I had this revelation. It's about time for me to start paying more attention to my skin, my face. Because you just don't realize how fast time passes." The Travel Channel provides the Lisbon forecast (high of 77) and then a documentary about Austria, a country you "may encounter on the far shores of the world, wherever humanity is striving to improve life." For instance, "airport passengers in Los Angeles may be driven to the terminal by airport buses made in Austria." The Hobel, a machine from nearby West Germany, is featured on *Breakthroughs.* It transforms food preparation from a tedious routine into an exciting event, and is top-rack-dishwasher-safe. Precision-minted pewter medallions celebrating former President Reagan are available for $10 on the Nashville Network. "Tums tastes like chalk," proclaims an ex–Tums user. On *McHale's Navy,* all leaves have been canceled until annoying enemy pilot Washing Machine Charlie can be silenced, much to McHale's disgust. ("If he's a menace, I'm a ring-tailed goony bird," he declares.) Hans, a Dutch national, prepares a creamy Gouda sauce to drizzle over cauliflower for the A&E audience. A harrowing documentary on the Howard University station documents the British genocide of Tasmanian aborigines, right down to the last man, whose skeleton hangs in the Oxford Museum. Richard Simmons introduces his brother, who used to weigh 205 pounds: "Here I was only forty-two and I felt fifty-two, maybe sixty-two." There's terrible flooding in Texas—on the *Today* show, a woman is plucked off the roof of her submerged car by a helicopter. Richard Nixon tells Bryant Gumbel that while it's true his resignation from the presidency may continue to cloud his record, "the main point is to live life to the hilt, all the time you possibly can, and to continue to give it your best shot to the end." Owning a firearm is a deeply personal decision, says a young woman in a checkered suit appearing on behalf of the NRA. "Whistle at me, will you, you shirt-tail cousin to a piccolo!" declares Wally Gator, "the swinging navigator in the swamp." A preacher is explaining something on the Inspirational Network—"As long as you're holding on to cash, you can't do anything with it. And if God tries to give you more, what happens?" He demonstrates—the bills bounce off your closed fist and fall to the floor. On the CBS morning news a "controversial Milwaukee alderman" says that unless a hundred-million-dollar minority jobs program is created soon, "revolutionary violence will be committed against the city of Milwaukee." Newly released hostage Frank Reed declares from his hospital balcony that he is looking forward to a three-pound Maine lobster. A man named Delvin Miller has been harness racing for eight decades, not including a stretch in World War II where he trained mules to deliver medicine in Burma for General "Vinegar Joe" Stilwell. The members of singing group Wilson Phillips remark that people tell them their name makes them sound like a law firm or a type of screwdriver. Fairfax County residents are encouraged to burlap-band their trees for gypsy-moth detection and control. "The reason I'll always make a big deal about three-quarters sleeves is that you always used to have to push up your sleeves," says an announcer on the J. C. Penney Channel. Hamstrings work in opposition to quadriceps, according to an exercise instructor on the Lifetime Channel, who adds "the adductor muscles are too tight in most of the population." More CEOs of Fortune 500 companies were born under Taurus than any other sign; also, age-based sizing for children's clothing is out-of-date because children are larger than they were when the sizing was devised. A National Family Opinion Research survey discussed on Channel 34 found that most consumers "aren't shy about testing out beds in retail showrooms." On MTV, Bruce Dickinson of Iron Maiden describes his new solo album, which has songs about how there are "all those people at the cocktail party with their little masks on, and all the businessmen in their suits and ties and they're just stabbing each other in the back all the time." (Adds Dickinson, "We've got a real rip-your-head-off direction in Maiden, and we're very proud of that direction. But with the solo stuff I can do stuff that's a little more varied.") Research from the University of Wisconsin indicates that hamburger may contain certain substances that inhibit skin cancer. Congressman Donald "Buz" Lukens, who was convicted of having sex with a sixteen-year-old, said he had made a "dumb mistake" but that he would run for reelection anyway.

By now it's nearly eight.

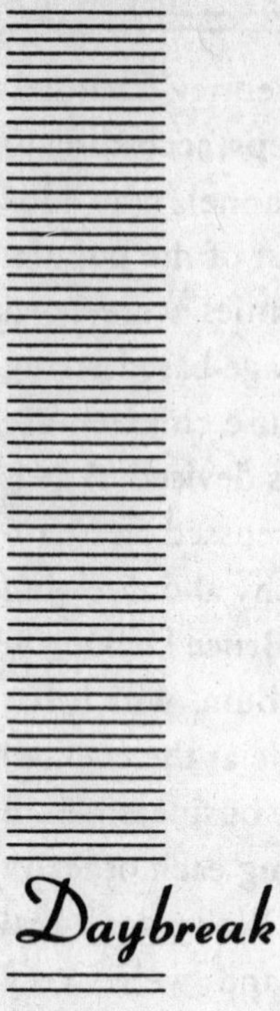

Daybreak

A little mist hangs above the pond, which is still save for a single mallard paddling slowly back and forth. From time to time it dives—sticks its rump in the air. From time to time it climbs out on a rock and airs its wings in the breeze, which is visible now and again on the surface of the pond. I watched for about an hour, and mostly the duck just swam back and forth, back and forth, back and forth.

Ducks are not necessarily placid. At certain times of the year male mallards flick water at females, or engage in what the bird books call a "grunt-whistle," while females perform "nod-swimming." At other seasons they may pull feathers from their bodies to insulate their eggs. And ducks are peculiarly susceptible to "imprinting." If, between thirteen and sixteen hours after they hatch, they are exposed to a moving object—a man or a dog or an Infiniti Q-45—they will thereafter follow it.

But on this particular morning this particular duck was doing nothing much, just swimming slowly back and forth.

We believe that we live in the "age of information," that there has been an information "explosion," an information "revolution." While in a certain narrow sense this is the case, in many important ways just the opposite is true. We also live at a moment of deep ignorance, when vital knowledge that humans have always possessed about who we are and where we live seems beyond our reach. An Unenlightenment. An age of missing information.

This account of that age takes the form of an experiment—a contrast between two days. One day, May 3, 1990, lasted well more than a thousand hours—I collected on videotape nearly every minute of television that came across the enormous Fairfax cable system from one morning to the next, and then I watched it all. The other day, later that summer, lasted the conventional twenty-four hours. A mile from my house, camped on a mountaintop by a small pond, I awoke, took a day hike up a neighboring peak, returned to the pond for a swim, made supper, and watched the stars till I fell asleep. This book is about the results of that experiment—about the information that each day imparted.

These are, of course, straw days. No one spends twenty-four hours a day watching television (though an impressive percentage of the population gives it their best shot). And almost no one spends much time alone outdoors—the hermit tradition, never strong in America, has all but died away. (Thoreau came up twice on television during May 3. Once, he was an answer on *Tic Tac Dough* in the category "Bearded Men," and later that evening, in the back of a limousine, a man toasted his fiancée with champagne and said, "You know how we've always talked about finding our Walden Pond, our own little utopia? Well, here it is. This is Falconcrest.") I'm not interested in deciding which of these ways of spending time is "better." Both are caricatures, and neither strikes me as a model for a full and happy life. But caricatures have their uses—they draw attention to what is important about the familiar. Our society is moving steadily from natural sources of information toward electronic ones, from the mountain and the field toward the television; this great transition is very nearly complete. And so we need to understand the two extremes. One is the target of our drift. The other an anchor that might tug us gently back, a source of information that once spoke clearly to us and now hardly even whispers.

About the mountain first. Crow Mountain is no Himalaya, no Alp. Even in the company of its fellow Adirondacks it keeps a low profile. It is not one of the fifty highest peaks in New York State, nor is it particularly difficult to climb—I was at the top with a two-hour hike from my back door. A day on Crow, then, offers little in the way of drama or danger or overcoming odds. Still, this mountain has its charms, including half a mile of bare ridge, with marvelous views in all directions, and an uncommonly large pond, perhaps ten acres in size, nestled just below the peak. It is an uncrowded summit—the day described here came at the end of a week I spent alone on Crow, a week in which I encountered no other human beings. And yet it is not isolated. From the ridge I could see down to the valley where my wife and I live—could see the volunteer firehouse and the few homes and grown-in pastures that form our community. Though my house was hidden behind a ridge of hemlock, I could see where Mill Creek twists through the yard. So Crow is wilderness softened by familiarity.

If climbing the mountain was easy, assembling a video record of May 3, 1990, was not. No machine exists that can tape nearly a hundred channels simultaneously; instead, you need a hundred people with videocassette recorders who will simultaneously do you a favor. With their help I compiled what I think is a unique snapshot of American culture—a sort of video Domesday that for twenty-four hours captures the images and voices that normally vanish like birdcalls on the breeze. For even in the age of the VCR, the invisible-ink effect of television is amazing. One day last year, for instance, a reporter for *The New York Times* needed to find out how the local ABC affiliate had covered a story the previous night. He failed, reporting only that a spokesman "could not release what was said on Sunday night's newscast without the permission of William Applegate, the news director, and Mr. Applegate did not respond to repeated requests left with his secretary for a transcript." In other words, the most powerful newspaper in the world could not get its hands on a newscast watched by millions only hours before. So I was pleased with my archive of tape, even if there were hours blanked out here and there, and MTV was nothing but snow so I had to retape it and a few others a couple of days later, and several hours of CBS were in black and white.

I chose Fairfax solely because of the astounding size of the system, which in 1990 was roughly 40 percent larger than its nearest competitor. There were five Christian channels, four shopping channels, two country music video channels, even a channel that broadcasts all the arrival and departure information off the Dulles and National airport screens. Its *Cable Guide* lists nearly a thousand movies each month; in May 1990 they ranged from *About Last Night* ("1986, Romantic Comedy, A young man and woman find themselves confused, frustrated, enthralled") to *Zombie* ("1964, Horror, Friends vacationing on a remote island find it inhabited by disfigured ghouls"), with everything in between from *Slumber Party Massacre II* to *The Son of Hercules Versus Medusa* to *It Happened One Night* to *Bonzo Goes to College* to *Sagebrush Law* to *Shaft* (and *Shaft in Africa*) to *Watchers* ("1988, Science Fiction, A dog, the subject of experiments in fostering superintelligence, escapes from a CIA compound"). For those who want *more,* a six-channel pay-per-view setup offers first-run films—on May 3: *Lethal Weapon 2; Honey, I Shrunk the Kids; Welcome Home; Field of Dreams; Alienator* ("She's programmed to kill anything in her path"); and *Enraptured.* Two comedy channels, nine public-access and government channels, a national sports channel and a local one, two weather channels, even a unique "four-in-one" channel that splits your screen into quarters and lets you watch the three networks and PBS simultaneously. Before the nineties are out, technology could permit six hundred channels per set, but even with a hundred stations you can watch virtually every national TV program aired in America on Fairfax Cable. On a single day you can hear about virtually every topic on earth.

Fairfax turned out to be ideal in another way, too—it is hard to imagine a place more devoid of quirky regional tradition. The county has grown quickly in recent years, till large stretches of it have the relentlessly standardized look of neutral America, the placeless Edge City of interchange plazas and malls with crowded chain restaurants and housing developments (Foxfield, Brookfield, Century Oak) named for the things they replaced. Only in its wealth is it extreme. The town of Falls Church ranks first in the nation in per capita income; nearly 80 percent of the county's households earn more than $35,000 and 75 percent of their children, who score seventy points above the national average on the SAT, will go on to college. On the other hand, a lot of the local programming comes from the District of Columbia, which is like a photographic negative of Fairfax.

Once my friends in Fairfax had mailed me the cardboard boxes full of tape, I began spending eight or ten hours a day in front of the VCR—I watched it all, more or less. A few programs repeat endlessly, with half-hour "infomercials" for DiDi 7 spot remover and Liquid Lustre car wax leading the list at more than a dozen appearances apiece. Having decided that once or twice was enough to mine their meanings, I would fast-forward through them, though I always slowed down to enjoy the part where the car-wax guy sets fire to the hood of his car. Otherwise, however, I dutifully spent many months of forty-hour weeks staring at, say, *Outdoors Wisconsin*, the kind of show that appears on minor cable channels across the nation because there's nowhere near enough programming produced to fill all the available time. On *Outdoors Wisconsin* ("summer to fall, winter to spring, Green Bay to where the St. Croix sings") they were "sucker-grabbing" in a creek near Fond du Lac. Sucker-grabbing involves wading up behind suckers, which are a variety of fish, and grabbing them. "They're really good if you grind 'em and mix 'em with a little egg and soda cracker," the host contended.

Which leads pretty directly into the question "Why bother?" *Outdoors Wisconsin* clearly has little direct effect on anyone but the suckers. But TV is cumulative, and over a lifetime ten minutes here and there of watching fishing or car racing or *Divorce Court* has added up to a lot of hours and had a certain effect on all of us. When people write about television, especially the critics who have to do it regularly, they usually have no choice but to concentrate on the new and the interesting as if they were reviewing plays or films. But TV is different—the new is relatively unimportant. The most popular program in 1990, *Cheers*, was in its ninth season; several weeks it was topped in the ratings by twenty-two-year-old *60 Minutes*, or challenged by *Murder, She Wrote*, which turned a hardy seven. Programs that first aired twenty or thirty years ago are still on the air, shown more often than ever in ceaseless rerun. You could argue that *The Brady Bunch*, not *Twin Peaks*, is the really important show to understand—simply by dint of repetition and familiarity it has won its way into the culture. (In March of 1991, the Associated Press reported that a Florida police officer had pleaded guilty to battery charges. He had lined up fourteen juveniles he had caught skateboarding, and then gone down the line whacking them with a nightstick as he sang the theme from *The Brady Bunch*. "He was singing that *Brady Bunch* tune, and each time he'd say like two words, he would hit one person in the butt," one of the boys told investigators.) People don't watch TV the way critics have to watch it. They don't watch it the way I watched it either—I have no way of re-creating the discussions the next day at work, say, or the easy familiarity with a show that you've seen every Thursday for a decade. But I did watch everything. The commercials, the filler, the reruns, the videos—all of it counts. *My Three Sons* still alters people's orbits, at least a little, just as Cosby will still be a force in 2010.

I grew up in the sixties and seventies, watching a great deal of television. Not the "quality TV" of television's Golden Era in the 1950s—not *Playhouse 90* or *The Honey-*

mooners. I was watching TV TV. Friday night meant ABC—*The Brady Bunch, The Partridge Family,* and *Room 222* in that order. TV was like a third parent—a source of ideas and information and impressions. And not such a bad parent—always with time to spare, always eager to please, often funny. TV filled dull hours and it made me a cosmopolite at an early age. I have great affection for it—I can remember waiting anxiously for *Room 222* to come on, remember that the high school it showed (Bernie with the red Afro! Karen Valentine!) seemed impossibly, enticingly sophisticated. People who didn't grow up with television tend not to understand its real power—they already had a real world to compare with the pictures on the screen. People my age didn't—we were steeped in television, flavored for life. A few years ago my wife and I moved to a mountain-rimmed valley—there's no cable, and even with a big antenna you get mostly snow. Since necessity is the mother of acquiescence, TV proved a fairly easy habit to kick. But of course I hadn't escaped it entirely—it lingered in my temperament, attitudes, outlook. And only with some distance, some time away, was I starting to get a sense of just how much. As I embarked on this project, then, I was not some Martian suddenly confronted with television; I was a traveler returning to a cozy home, able to see that home with new eyes. Going back to television was like spending the holidays with your parents once you've grown up—in three days you comprehend more on a conscious level about your mother than you did in twenty years of living with her.

Only in part is this a book *about* television; often I will be describing phenomena that appear *on* television but also on the radio and in magazines and everywhere else, because they are parts of modern life. The amount of territory that television covers in twenty-four hours is extraordinary—I could find fifty references to any topic that interested me. TV is a pipeline to the modern world, and a convenient shorthand for some of its features. Still, that does not mean that TV *merely* reflects our society. By virtue of its omnipresence, it also constantly reinforces certain ideas. It is less an art form than the outlet for a utility—like the faucet on a sink that connects you to the river, the TV links you to a ceaselessly flowing stream of information, and that very ceaselessness makes it different from a play or a movie. Television is the chief way that most of us partake of the larger world, of the information age, and so, though none of us owe our personalities and habits entirely to the tube and the world it shows, none of us completely escape its influence either. Why do we do the things we do? Because of the events of our childhood, and because of class and race and gender, and because of our political and economic system and because of "human nature"—but also because of what we've been told about the world, because of the information we've received. That's why for me the biggest question is not if the world before TV was a better place or if TV leads to violence. Nor for the purposes of this book do I much care if television is manipulated by giant corporations, the military-industrial complex, the "pressure of ratings," the hidden power of

Freemasonry, or the signs of the zodiac. These are important questions, but they're not my question. My question is "What's on?"

Television researchers tend to ignore the content, taking their cue from Marshall McLuhan, who argued that the "content of a medium is like the juicy meat piece of meat carried by the burglar to distract the watchdog of the mind." One study after another, not to mention the experience of most of us, indicates that McLuhan was largely right—that we do in fact often watch television because of our mood or out of habit, instead of tuning in to see something in particular. Even so, we're not staring at test patterns. We also often eat because we're bored or depressed, but the effects are different if we scarf carrot sticks or Doritos.

Two thirds of Americans tell researchers they get "most of their information" about the world from television, and the other statistics are so familiar we hardly notice them—more American homes have TVs than plumbing and they're on an average of seven hours a day; children spend more time watching TV than doing anything else save sleeping; on weekday evenings in the winter half the American population is sitting in front of television; as many as 12 percent of adults (that is, one in eight) feel they are physically addicted to the set, watching an average of fifty-six hours a week; and so on. The industry works hard to make this absorption seem glamorous: the Fairfax system runs an around-the-clock Cable Welcome Channel for instance, which tells viewers how to operate their systems ("If you can't get a picture on your TV, make sure it is plugged in"), but mainly congratulates them endlessly on "being part of a complete communications system that puts the whole world at your fingertips, from the far reaches of outer space to the heart of Fairfax." Outer space! Satellites! Fiber optics! Data! The final installment of an A&E series called *The Romantic Spirit* gushes, "Computers and satellites and silicon chips signal that we are in sight of a post–Romantic Age, of a fresh start." Communications are now "almost instantaneous," a documentary on the computer age explains. "Communications are the currency we trade in, the currency of the information age."

But what is this vaunted information currency? If you're a commodity broker or a bond trader, it's a blizzard of constantly changing green numbers on a flashing screen. If you're a vice president for marketing, it's a cataract of data about how much people earn in a certain zip code and what kind of car they drive. For most of us, though, this romantic, mind-boggling Niagara of communications washes up in our living rooms in the form of, say, Cory Everson's hunky husband, Jeff. Cory has an exercise program on ESPN called *Body Shaping,* and she lets Jeff handle the show's Nutrition Corner. If you're in the supermarket, Jeff advises, and you open up a carton and see that one of the eggs is broken, "don't buy that carton."

To be fair, there's a lot of other information you didn't already know, some of which is vaguely fascinating. On the Discovery Channel, for instance, Dr. Frank Field explains that in Switzerland white bread is taxed and the money is given to whole-wheat bakers so their loaves can be competitively priced. According to Casey Kasem on *Oprah,*

Neil Sedaka went to the same high school as Neil Diamond and Barbra Streisand, and while he was there he wrote a song about a girl called Carole Klein who went on to become Carole King and of course have several number-one records, not only for herself but for the Shirelles. Sea otters wrap themselves in kelp before going to sleep, and three thousand matings are required to produce one lion cub that will live past its second year, and hyenas usually bear twins. And according to Showtime, the Voyager space probe carries a recording offering our planet's greetings to the entire universe in the voice of—Kurt Waldheim.

Some of the information on TV could win you fabulous prizes. "In American literature, what Mark Twain character had a girlfriend named Becky Thatcher?" As English teachers across the nation held their collective breath, a team on *Super Sloppy Double Dare* who had earlier recalled the name of the Flintstones' pet dinosaur failed to remember Tom Sawyer, and so had to turn themselves into "human tacos" by pouring vats of guacamole on their heads.

On other occasions, the information is more speculative: John Osborne, in a special edition of *Prophecy Countdown* called "Angels—God's Special Space Shuttles," calculated that angels travel eleven million miles a minute versus 283 for a NASA rocket.

And once in a while the information is just a shade less than honest, as when the Travel Channel claimed that "three things make Nuremberg famous—its Christmas market, the Nuremberg gingerbread, and the Nuremberg sausage."

Most of the time, though, the information that TV has to offer is not spelled out in such tidy little factlets. It is at at least a little hidden in the fabric of movies and newscasts and commercials and reruns. Not so hidden that you need to hire a team of deconstruction contractors to analyze it all—just hidden enough that the messages are passed over, absorbed through the eyes without triggering the entire brain. People used to claim you could see "sex" written on Ritz crackers in their advertisements. Despite careful examination I never could, and that's not what I'm talking about. What I'm talking about is what happens when you see an ad, over and over, for small Ritz crackers pre-smeared and pre-stuck together with peanut butter and sold under the slogan "No assembly required." What habits of mind and body does this, in concert with a hundred other similar messages, help produce? And how do those habits differ from the habits, the attitudes people got from the natural world?

Occasionally, in between old World War II documentaries on A&E, a promotion for the network showed a man named Jack Perkins who said proudly that his channel showed "the entire scope of television, which is of course the entire scope of life." This is more or less the claim of all those who herald the new age now upon us—that our flow of data replaces nearly all that came before, including nature. Mark Fowler, the Reagan-era director of the Federal Communications Commission, appeared on C-SPAN to make this point explicitly. He talked about the range of environmental problems we face, including the depletion of the ozone, the destruction of the rain forests, and the spread of acid rain. "Pretty dreary stuff," he said, "except that as the ecological system has deteriorated, I think the man-made information ecology—the ebb and flow of words, voice, data—has vastly improved, so that we now live in a world more tightly bound, more in touch one part with another, than at any moment in its history."

Set aside the question of whether it's a worthwhile trade-off to be able to fax your aunt in Australia so that you can tell her it's bloody hot out and all the fish are dying—simply realize that an awful lot of people have come to see this "information ecology" as a sort of substitute for the other, older, natural ecology. "Ours is an economy increasingly dependent not on our natural resources or geographic location," President Bush told the members of the class of 1991 as they left the California Institute of Technology. "Ours is an age of microchips and MTV." And most of us vaguely agree with the president, I think—the world seems to be evolving into an "information economy" where the occupants of every country will busy themselves selling each other computer chips and watching the whole process on Esperanto CNN.

Against such a tide of opinion it sounds a little romantic to say: If you sat by a pond beside a hemlock tree under the sun and stars for a day, you might acquire some information that would serve you well. I don't fret about TV because it's decadent or shortens your attention span or leads to murder. It worries me because it alters perception. TV, and the culture it anchors, masks and drowns out the subtle and vital information contact with the real world once provided. There are lessons—small lessons, enormous lessons, lessons that may be crucial to the planet's persistence as a green and diverse place and also to the happiness of its inhabitants—that nature teaches and TV can't. Subversive ideas about how much you need, or what comfort is, or beauty, or time, that you can learn from the one great logoless channel and not the hundred noisy ones or even the pay-per-view.

For instance, as the sun comes up I'm sitting by the edge of the pond on Crow, drinking tea and wondering idly if the weather will hold all day so I can hike to the cliffs on nearby Blackberry Mountain. Ransacking my brain for weather lore, I recall that red skies at night are a sailor's delight, a ring around the moon heralds snow, and woolly caterpillars are woolliest before a hard winter, none of which is much help. I find myself wishing that I could gauge the wind direction and its speed, add the feel of the air and the type of clouds overhead, and make a reasonable guess, as most Americans once could, of what the day would bring. Of course this is no longer an essential skill—on the Fairfax cable system alone you can watch not only the twenty-four-hour national Weather Channel but also a local radar weather channel that shows storms moving inexorably, pixel by pixel, in your direction. You'd be crazy to devote any time to learning to forecast from the clouds and the wind—you wouldn't be as accurate as the giggly guy in the loud sports coat, and who would teach you anyhow? Jeffersonian farmers would doubtless have welcomed accurate predictions. Still, let this stand as one small example of information people once had and no longer possess.

Or another small example: an oft-repeated ad on May 3 was for a product called Jimmy Dean Microwave Mini Burgers, prefabricated hamburgers in a microwavable container. Silly as it sounds, think of the information you would have needed a century ago if you lived in a place like the Adirondacks and wanted to make yourself a hamburger. You'd have needed to be able to raise cattle, which implies knowing how to clear land, how to rotate pastures, how to build a barn—probably you'd have needed to know how to get your neighbors to *help* you raise a barn. You'd have needed to know how to kill an animal, and what to do with it once it was hanging there dead. You might have bought your grain at the store or you might have used cornmeal, but certainly you needed to know how to bake bread. Baking and cooking would have required wood, which meant you had to know which trees to cut down, and when, and how to build an even fire. And so on.

I do not mean that this was a more virtuous way to produce a hamburger, or that there's something effete about learning the weather from Willard Scott. Clearly, TV is not to blame for these developments; it merely chronicles them. And these particular skills, in and of themselves, may not be so important. However, in the course of performing them, one could not help accumulating a large store of what you could call "fundamental" information, and it is precisely this kind of fundamental information I want to rediscover in this book. I went to the mountains to get it—until recently, though, it was more routinely obtained, more a part of everyday life.

During most of human history, this fundamental information came most of all from agriculture. The vast majority of people lived on farms, of course—only a century ago most Americans still lived in rural areas. Now farmers are an anachronism. We tend to think of them in sentimental terms, as virtuous, but also vaguely embarrassing. When ESPN broadcast the world horseshoe-pitching championship (an up-and-coming event that surely soon will be the Miller Genuine Draft Pro World Pitching Championship), an official of the sport's governing body felt compelled to say: "A lot of people still have that image of horseshoe pitchers being farmers in bib overalls. But that's really a misnomer. Here at the world tournament, less than one percent of our entrants are what you might call farmers. Some are ranchers, but we have a good cross-section of professional people—doctors, lawyers, mathematicians, teachers, physicists even." Or listen to Marshall McLuhan. In the middle of one of his usual riffs about the glories of the "electronically configured world . . . a world not of wheels but of circuits, not of fragments but of integral patterns," he recounted a conversation he had with an executive at IBM. "My children," the man told McLuhan, "had lived several lifetimes compared to their grandparents when they began grade one."

Which, basically, is nonsense. While McLuhan's idealized youth may have reams of data unavailable to the wisest adult of a few generations earlier, they had much less access to precisely the kinds of fundamental information we most sorely lack. Even the dullest farmer quickly learns, for instance, a deep sense of limits. You can't harvest crops successfully until you understand how much can be grown without exhausting the soil, how much rest the land requires, which fields can be safely plowed and which are so erosion-prone they're best left to some other purpose. This sense of the limits of one particular place grants you some sense that the world as a whole has limits, a piece of information we've largely forgotten, in part because being a successful businessperson involves constantly breaking through limits. Instead of learning about limits before they reach kindergarten, kids watch, say, *The Gobots,* a cartoon assemblage that turn from robots into late-model automobiles and back again. On this day they unveiled a new invention: a "proton cultivator that will solve the problems of feeding the people of the earth. It will make barren land fertile"—indeed a single dose turned cartoon desert to cartoon corn. Losing this sense of limits matters—one reason we're so blithe about doubling the present population of the world must be that we think some such device will double the amount of food we grow. (Between 1985 and 1990, in truth, the world's per capita production of calories declined.)

If we're ever to recapture these fundamental kinds of information, it's necessary to start by remembering just how divorced from the physical world many of us have become. In a refreshingly honest piece of reporting, food writer Dena Kleiman recently told readers of *The New York Times* about a trip she'd taken to the lake district of southern Chile. "I had always fantasized about eating my own catch—staring down at a plate of fresh fish and knowing it would never have got there without me. The whole idea was appealing: braving the elements, testing my skill, indulging in one of the oldest battles of time—man versus nature." So she jumped at the chance to go fishing in Chile, although not before consulting with a passel of experts. George J. Armelagos, an anthropologist at the University of Florida, told her that "it was not until about ten thousand years ago that humans first turned from hunting and fishing to farming and herding in what was the start of the Neolithic Age." After that "nothing was ever the same," explained Mr. Armelagos, who is also the author of *Consuming Passions: An Anthology of Eating.* Ultimately, added California anthropology professor Eugene Anderson, "it is capitalism that has distanced us from all stages and phases of the food preparation process." Having heard this, Kleiman was ready. The management of the hotel sent her off in a boat with a guide, and the chef promised he would sauté her catch with a touch of garlic. "Time passes slowly in a fishing boat," she reported. "The routine, in fact, is tedious. Cast out. Reel in." To fill the time, "I tried to envision what kind of weapon I would devise, what kind of skill might be required, what kind of mind-set I would need to develop if I were lost in the wilderness and confronted with starvation." While mulling over this problem, she caught a fish, the guide motored her in, and she handed it to the chef and dressed for dinner. But presented with her catch, she reports, "I was stunned to find myself suddenly feeling nauseated," unable to eat for the memory of the vibrant living creature of some hours before. Despite the assurances of one Robert Cialdini, a social psychologist at the University of Arizona, that "it is natural for us to generate food for ourselves," she went without her supper.

Her squeamishness is not the point—that may be her only natural reaction, and in any event it's not deep enough to stop her eating the flesh of animals she didn't catch herself. It's how profoundly disconnected an obviously intelligent and educated person can be from the natural world. She is perhaps a slight caricature in this regard—only a true Manhattanite would actually consult a professor for the news that it is okay for us to "generate" our own food—but she offers a pretty accurate drawing of our society as a whole. Even most of us who do hike and fish do so sporadically, and out of such a single-minded desire for recreation that we don't absorb a lot of meaning from the experience. What you do every day, after all, is what forms your mind, and precious few of us can or would spend most days outdoors. "Despite all the lip service we give to craving nature and wanting to spend more time away from cities, I suppose that in the end we are grateful to live in a society where foraging requires only a walk to the local market," Kleiman writes. And that is fine—we don't need a nation of hunter-gatherers. But it does, as she demonstrates, come at a real cost in your comprehension of the world—it robs her of the ability, in this instance, to squarely address her own participation in the drama of life and death.

Even for the few modern farmers who do appear on television, the industrial scale of the business has changed it so dramatically that much of this information is diluted, drowned out in the roar of the tractor piloting its noisy course across a vast sea of crops. The Lifetime network ran a short feature on a farm family in northern California. They ran such a large dairy operation (950 head) that the mother said she spent most of her day on the computer doing records while Dad was out minding the help. The kids took care of the house pets, and helped in other small ways, but they weren't really a part of farm life any more than a banker's children make loans. The message she tried to teach them, Mom said, was that "hard work pays off in nice things—toys, cars." Which is probably better than our culture's usual message—Buy a lottery ticket so you won't have to work hard—but it doesn't yield much in the way of wisdom about death or limits or the cycles of the seasons. Even home gardeners, presumably planting for love of working the soil, are hectored around the clock to purchase products like Miracle-Gro—hectored by "world championship gardeners," which is to say not the people who grow the tastiest vegetables or produce them most thriftily, or with the most care for their soils. No, these are the people who through constant application of chemicals have managed to produce the *largest* vegetables, great pulpy squashes and melons.

The narrow valley at the foot of Crow Mountain was once a farm—we know how grand it looked because a poet, Jeanne Robert Foster, lived in the mountain's shadow as a girl. But the farmer who had built it watched as his children left for other, shinier pursuits. An old man, he looked on in despair as his fields began the slow return to forest:

I must find a man who still loves the soil
Walk by his side unseen, pour in his mind
What I loved when I lived until he builds
Sows, reaps, and covers these hill pastures here
With sheep and cattle, mows the meadowland
Grafts the old orchard again, makes it bear again
Knowing that we are lost if the land does not yield.

As I stand on the ridge this morning, looking at the sumac and the birch covering the pasture, it is clear he never found his man. And clear that most of us will need some way other than a life of growing crops to get at this fundamental information.

There are other paths to this kind of deeper understanding of the world, but they too are overgrown and hard to find; a day of watching television makes it obvious that farming is not the only skill we've lost. Often, in fact, the television culture celebrates incompetence. One American Express ad depicts a couple who have chartered a sailboat in the tropics but are having a difficult time operating it. Suddenly they see a cruise schooner round the point, and to the triumphant Big Chill strains of "Rescue Me" they ditch their scow and jump aboard the luxury yacht, where there's a crew to attend to stuff like *sails* and *wind* and *lines* and *rocks* so they can concentrate on drinking. Money supplants skill; its possession allows us to become happily stupid. Presumably the crew members on the yacht make enough money pursuing *their* specialty that they don't need to know about anything else themselves either. Certainly most TV characters don't possess many skills; except for tending bar and solving murders, virtually no one in a drama or comedy actually works.

Occasionally, though, television offers a few glimpses of people who have developed very deep mastery, become real craftsmen. There are baseball games (on this evening the Braves were losing to the Pirates) where you get to watch men employ an enormous accretion of specialized knowledge—"There's a good hitter's pitch coming here," "He's shading him to right." On public TV, a man demonstrated the art of Chinese calligraphy. And off in the back alleys of cable there are a great many cooking shows run by chefs who can chop, whisk, separate, fold, knead, and roll, all in a blur.

These kinds of skills come from long, repetitive, and disciplined apprenticeships. Societies have always, at least since the beginning of agriculture, needed and valued certain specialized abilities; while the great majority of people were learning from their parents to produce food and otherwise care for themselves, a few were spending years with a master of some craft or art. Where the one education was broad, the other was deep—deeper, say, than law school. *So* deep that it may have produced some of the same kinds of fundamental knowledge that farming produces, because the master taught not just cooking or painting but universal things. As the poet and longtime Buddhist novice Gary Snyder wrote recently, "The youngsters left home to go and sleep in the back of the potting shed and would be given the single task of mixing clay for three years. . . . It was understood that the teacher would test one's patience and fortitude endlessly. One could not think of turning back, but just take it, go deep, and have no other interests." In the TV era, we're more comfortable with, say, Robert Warren, who has a cable art show and today is teaching all of America how to paint "Majestic Mountain Meadow." No three seasons of watching Robert mix paints! Or perhaps the amazing piano course sold by former Detroit Lion Alex Karras and endorsed by Davy Jones—"Now the Monkees can play their own instruments." Or maybe you'd like the Paint by Numbers Last Supper Painting Kit from the QVC shopping channel. "Duplicate Leonardo da Vinci's beautiful painting—you get 42 shades, so many that you're going to get very close to da Vinci. . . . You'll be able to learn just what goes into making an intricate painting like this. Give yourself the pride of accomplishment."

Still, there are echoes. The notion of apprenticeship as an almost religious vocation survives best, oddly, in martial arts movies like *Bloodsport* on Showtime. Representative of its type, it featured a young Caucasian who had studied for many years under a Japanese master. His command of body and soul was complete—he had reached the point where he fought not for external reward (for the teacher gave none, not even a smile) or for his liking for blood (he hated it—his master left Japan after his family was killed at Hiroshima). Instead he fought for an essentially spiritual satisfaction—because it made him feel close to some universal force. We thrill to this in part because it's a ridiculous excuse to let people kick each other's teeth in. But there's also something deeply attractive about that depth of training, that self-abnegation. We secretly believe that people who have gone through it *may* understand more about who they are. *Bloodsport* was followed on Showtime by Championship Boxing (Michael "The Silk" Olaajide losing a decision to Thomas "Hitman" Hearns). In an even more degraded way, boxing is about the same kind of issues. The great dramas in the sport only occasionally take place in the ring—usually they're outside it, where we watch to see if young men "stick to their training" or at the first flush of victory begin buying Italian cars and fancy women and letting their hangers-on coax them into staying up late at night. That is, will they trade their secrets and their discipline for the glitter of the world? Almost invariably flash wins out, in part because by old master-apprentice standards the training is not very rigorous (and because most other sorts of apprentices don't make $20 million a year). Still, we always find ourselves hoping.

Handcrafting pottery and samurai fighting and growing corn may be outmoded skills, but perhaps all the discipline and wisdom they offer can be acquired through more modern devotions, in which case my day on the mountain would be unnecessary. That is one of the arguments Robert Pirsig makes in *Zen and the Art of Motorcycle Maintenance* when he says "the Buddha, the Godhead, resides quite as comfortably in the circuits of a digital computer or the gears of a cycle transmission as he does at the top of a mountain or in the petals of a flower." ("I am master of my fate, captain of my soul," intones an ad for BMW motorcycles.) The Buddha, for all I know, *is* as comfortable in the gearbox, but he's increasingly inaccessible. Albert Borgmann, in a book called *Technology and the Character of Contemporary Life*, argues convincingly that Pirsig's approach becomes less and less helpful as technology progresses. When Pirsig wrote his book, a motorcycle was essentially a mechanical device; with each passing year it becomes more and more a microelectronic one, and you can't sit by the road and find God by looking at a bunch of incomprehensibly microscopic silicon chips. (You also can't repair your motorcycle anymore.) TV itself began as a toy for hobbyists, a gee-whiz gadget to build in the basement. Now it is too complex even for individual corporations—great manufacturing combines are getting together to develop High Definition TV. The great push is always *away* from individual skill and engagement—a horse took all sorts of information and insight to handle, and a Model T a little, and a Honda Accord virtually none.

It's a comfortable notion that as we progress we simply add to our store of understanding about the world—that we know more about the world by kindergarten than our grandparents knew when they died, and that our grandchildren will in turn be infinitely wiser than we are. In truth, though, we usually learn a new way of doing things at the expense of the old way. In this case we've traded away most of our physical sense of the world, and with it a whole category of information, of understanding. We have a new understanding, reflected most ubiquitously by television, which in many ways is sophisticated and powerful. And democratic—TV's obvious virtues, that it is cheap and always accessible—should not be overlooked. But there's much that it leaves out, that it can't include.

For only a few people anymore will this other information come from farming, and I don't anticipate a sudden, statistically significant boom in pot-throwing apprenticeships. So I'll concentrate on contrasting television's message with the ideas about the world and our place in it that come from a day in the natural world. In a way, I suppose, I'm hunting for a shortcut, which is the curse of the age. But it's a useful shortcut, since though few of us will farm, most people can still manage regular excursions into the natural world. It's not elitist—it's subversively easy.

To pull in this broadest of broadcasts you do not need pristine wilderness—there's very little, perhaps nothing, left that's entirely "natural." A city park or a suburban woodlot or a rural hedgegrow or a backyard garden will do—anyplace that will let you take a conscious step away from the entirely man-made world. In all these places you can read what John Muir called "the inexhaustible pages of nature . . . written over and over uncountable times, written in characters of every size and color, sentences composed of sentences, every part of a character a sentence."

That this broadcast has gone on since the start of time—that some of its messages still live in our genes and instincts—does not mean, however, that it will go on forever. Parts of Muir's grammar are wiped off the slate each day—species lost, ecosystems altered. You have to listen harder to the natural world so you can separate out the primal song from the songs of our civilization and from our static. A team of Canadian scientists recently finished a study of several lakes in a remote part of northern Ontario, an area where the temperature had increased 3.5 degrees in the last two decades—the kind of warming that other scientists tell us the whole planet can expect in the next two generations. The Canadian researchers reported all sorts of highly complex alterations of the environment. Warmer air had meant more evaporation, for instance. Hence, stream flows dropped and the lakes became clearer and therefore warmer. As a result, many cold-water species, including trout, faced extinction. But beyond their practical impact, the changes were simply one more sign that Muir's alphabet was turning into indecipherable hieroglyphics—one more sign that the great simplification had begun.

Much of this simplification may be irreversible. If so, we had best listen closely, since we will not get another chance. And what chance we *do* have of preserving this natural world also depends on listening—on absorbing the information of the mountain and garden and park as thoroughly as we soak up the information on the screen. And on letting it play as large a role in shaping the way we live. It depends, that is, on turning the present moment into a true age of information.

Midmorning

The heat of the day had nearly come, and I was lying on a shelf of rock by the pond when a plane, the only one that day, droned directly overhead, about three thousand feet above me. It was the daily flight from Albany to northern New York, a ten-seater I've flown several times. It offers a magnificent view of the entire Adirondacks, following the Hudson and then darting through the high mountain passes.

As I watched, it occurred to me that one of the questions that most needed answering, one of the crucial pieces of information I was seeking, was: Where do I live? In the human-scale world around me on the mountain and in the neighborhood I can see from the ridge? In the region as seen from the small plane, in my case the mountains and woody uplands of the Northeast? On the continents and hemispheres now spanned in a few hours by the bigger jets? Or on the spinning globe, as viewed from space? Some of all, obviously—but the constant implication of our time, sold with particular persuasiveness by the electronic media, is that the local and the regional matter less and less and the national and the global more and more.

Buckminster Fuller may top the list of modern prophets—writing with the velocity of a romance novelist, he poured out an endlessly shining vision of the human future. True, he was a bit of a crank—but he knew what direction we were heading, and he spurred us onward. "I travel between Southern and Northern hemispheres and around the world so frequently that I no longer have any so-called normal winter and summer, nor normal night and day, for I fly in and out of the shaded or sun-flooded areas of the spinning Earth with every increased frequency," he wrote exultantly. "I wear three watches. One is to tell me what time it is at my 'home' office, so that I can call them by long-distance telephone. One is set for the time of day in the place to which I am next going, and one is set temporarily for the locality in which I happen to be. I now see the earth realistically as a sphere and think of it as a spaceship."

Most of us, of course, don't spend our lives in airplanes on the way to give speeches, but we get to experience this boundless world ourselves just by flipping the switch—

"the whole world at your fingertips, from the far reaches of space to the heart of Fairfax." Ted Turner, creator of Cable News network and the incarnation of the Information Revolution, gave an address on C-SPAN on May 3 that centered on just this theme. "We have small fines at CNN to eliminate the word 'foreign' when talking about other nations and other individuals on this planet," he said. "I think we're all neighbors. Instead of 'foreign' affairs, 'international' affairs. The word 'foreign' has bad connotations because it says 'somewhere else.' Now, hundreds and thousands of years ago there *were* foreign countries. Even here, California was foreign to the East Coast because it took a year to get there." But now—now you can turn on American TV and see a program called *European Journal*, reporting on the World Championship of Freestyle Latin American Dance from Hamburg. The dance floor, ringed with advertising placards for MasterCard, tingles with controversy—the Scots have won by a tenth of a point over the crowd-favorite Germans. There don't seem to be any actual Latin Americans, but there is a sweet-looking couple from San Diego. "The Americans are slowly catching up to the European level of dancing," the announcer says, "but it will be some time before they achieve world titles."

When it first happened, this linking up of the world must have seemed profoundly glamorous. As chance would have it, the Nostalgia network was showing a 1941 musical—John Payne, Alice Faye, and Cesar Romero in *The Great American Broadcast.* A story of the early days of radio, it depicted the first remote broadcast (a Dempsey fight), and the quick growth of the wireless hobby—people were flushed with excitement because they'd picked up *Buffalo* on their crystal sets. The triumphant finale comes from the studio where the first nationwide broadcast is taking place, the showstopping number sung before a huge map of America with a light for every town with a receiving station. It *must* have been remarkable even the hundredth time that happened—when people who had previously been able to hear only from their neighbors suddenly could listen to the nation. Jeanne Robert Foster, the Crow Mountain poet, writes about moving to town as a girl, and looking up at the telegraph wires "that my father had told me girdled the earth, everywhere carrying power and dominion. As my father lifted me down from the load, the realization came for the first time that I, little unknown country maid of dolls and pinafores, was a part of the 'whole,' a part of this same 'power and dominion,' and I was ecstatically happy." By my youth, when all this was taken for granted, the whole notion got another boost from those photos the astronauts took of our planet, that blue-and-white orb sailing slowly through the vastness of space. "She is a fragile world adrift in a cosmic sea, mother of life and home to all living things. Rediscover Planet Earth tonight at ten," the Discovery Channel urges.

This is by no means all to the bad—she *is* a fragile world, and more and more we must learn to take some responsibility for the planet as a singular whole. But in the thrall of our new insight we forget that the planet also consists of diverse localnesses. Now that we are told each day that the earth is round, we've forgotten that it's also flat—local, small, particular. Television tells us we have everything in common. But we don't. And as we lose our particularity we lose prodigious amounts of information.

The most obvious drain is in our ecological understanding. Each piece of land the world over is different—the climate and the topography and the vegetation all combine to mean that the field over there is particularly vulnerable to erosion or that the deer need that bit of stream or that the groundwater's shallow here and easily depleted. These kinds of lessons—and the affection needed to implement them—can be learned only by long observation. From the ridge on Crow I can see most of the few dozen houses in my town. They're where they are for some physical reason—the creek drops there, so it was a natural place for a sawmill; there the valley floor broadens enough for a farm. The sawmill is gone and the pasture is growing in, but there's still some logic to the layout, some information provided by the topography and the soil. But farther in the distance I can see the spot where a new set of luxury vacation condos will be built next year, right on the edge of a gorgeous but tiny pond. The condos are not placed there for any physical reason save proximity to the ski hill and the increased value of "waterfront," and they're going to be pushed in one on another as close as the landscaping will allow. They will tell their inhabitants and their visitors nothing about the land—they are "machines for living," albeit inefficient ones, and quite possibly they will overwhelm that small pond, filling it with enough nitrogen that it chokes with algae and then dies. Those houses exist only in a brochure and a spiel, not in a place—they're like the houses advertised ceaselessly on Fairfax's real estate channel, whose locations refer only to the human world—"near the mall," "on a cul de sac." Such obliviousness to place exists around the developed world.

If you were really aware of living, say in Denver, as opposed to in "America" or in "affluence" or in "suburbia," you would not insist on having a green-grass lawn like some long-ago Sussex lord. You would have an appropriate—and beautiful—dry yard. But since Denver as a latitude and a longitude and an altitude and a vegetation zone means little to its residents, they dam great rivers so they can sprinkle, flood gorges so they can golf.

We tend to recognize this loss of information, of localness, more in cultural than in environmental terms. Once in a great while someone comes on TV speaking in a distinct regional accent, and you suddenly realize how rare it is—they tend to be country singers or poor people who have been unexpectedly caught in natural disasters (like the woman in flood-stricken Eufaula, Oklahoma, who said, "The house is ruint, the floor is ruint, so I guess we'll just have to find another place to live"). Also elderly Southern politicians, and rap musicians such as D-Nice, who appeared on *Yo, MTV Raps.* He held up a New York subway map and sang, "I live in the Bronx, by the D and the 4—Writing lyrics is addictive, writing more and more." But these are rare exceptions. In all these hundreds and thousands of hours of TV, the only reminder that Fairfax County sits south of the Mason-Dixon line was an advertisement for a product called Goody's Headache Powder—"The Number One Headache Powder in the South."

To call all this "information" may seem a grand use of

the term, but consider—our vast abundance of arts and necessities, from music to cooking, depends on an earlier period when people in particular places mastered their particular conditions. That is, the man who does the Cajun cooking show is the direct descendant of people who had, by virtue of the climate and terrain, lots of crawfish and spices and not much else. His forebears couldn't go shopping for fish with the Winn-Dixie marketing experts who appeared on the Nashville network's *American Magazine* with fresh marlin from the Gulf, catfish from a Mississippi catfish farm, ocean perch from the Atlantic, whiting from Argentina, and orange roughy ("the new fad fish") from New Zealand. His forebears had crawfish and they had whatever else the bayou and their garden patches provided, and so they went deep and really learned what there was to do with them. Here in the Adirondacks, if you were lucky you might have found an orange in your Christmas stocking. But apples! Jeanne Robert Foster wrote a poem about a local Johnny Appleseed, and just the names of the endless varieties make your mouth pucker: Seek-No-Furthers and Gill Flowers and Greenings, Tolman sweets and Russets, pippins and spice apples. "If you had a Sheep's Nose he'd pick that one / First of all, for he wanted to get seeds."

Seed savers and ethnomusicologists and oral historians have worked hard to preserve this kind of knowledge, but the great bulk of it has surely been lost as place has become unimportant to all but the old. The deep sense of ambivalence we feel about all of this was clear to me after I'd spent twenty-four hours watching the Travel Channel. On the one hand, it is the Buckminster Fuller of networks, complete with spinning-globe logo. Experts advise ceaselessly about avoiding jet lag (go to bed early, starting five days in advance) and talk about cruises where you hardly have to go on deck because there are so many resident bridge pros. However, the channel simultaneously conveys the strong sense that what you *really* want to see when you go abroad is *differences,* people living lives in interesting, un-American ways. When you go to Majorca, said one announcer, "I bet the things you remember are not the lively resorts but the quiet places that lie behind them." The next documentary promised that "another sort of Spain is waiting to be discovered if you take the trouble to travel beyond the beaches—an older, calmer Spain." We're starved for impressions, curious about how people live their lives who don't inhabit the great suburban sameness. As long as we stay in the big beachfront hotels all we can see is how *we* live our lives, though maybe more luxuriously and probably with more liquor. But we're so used to this way of life that it's hard and scary for most people to surrender it even for a day or two. This tug-of-war is reflected in the introductions to nearly all the travel documentaries that run day and night on the Travel Channel: "India, a country as wedded to the past as it is committed to the future"; "From the palaces of the Spanish conquerors to the sleek luxury hotels"; "Peru is a land of primitive beauty and stark contrast, where echoes of a far distant past can still be heard in ancient cities and villages, but the metropolis moves to a modern beat."

. . .

One idea—one phrase, really—casts a long shadow over this discussion. The notion that we live in a "global village" was first put forward by Marshall McLuhan in the 1960s. "Today after more than a century of electric technology we have extended our central nervous system itself in a global embrace abolishing both space and time as far as our planet is concerned," he wrote. "The new electric interdependence recreates the world in the image of a global village." In the decades since the resonant phrase "global village" has become a mighty cliché, repeated so often that we believe it to be true without really thinking about it. And what an attractive idea—it seems to solve the problem I've posed here. On the one hand we can follow the modern, commercial, political impulse toward globalization, toward standardization—and in the process create the intimacy of a village, the kind of close and connected personal and cultural life we've been vaguely missing. It sounds awfully good for other reasons too. It sounds like the way we're going to solve our worst political problems, so many of which (the environment, nuclear weapons) are global in scale. And in this image, quite explicitly, the TV is a sort of campfire, and also a set of jungle drums bearing the news.

Now, McLuhan said a lot of things, and some of them were clearly nonsense—he once described a thermonuclear explosion as "information," and he had complicated theories about how the flicker on a TV screen made it "low-definition" and therefore "participatory." (This was pre-Trinitron, and definitely before the TBS slam cam, which all evening offered wondrous microscopic close-ups of Hakeem Olajuwon throwing down monstrous dunks during the NBA playoffs.) Sometimes McLuhan was wronger than wrong, as when he predicted that "the TV image has ended the consumer phase of American culture." Always he was hailed too highly: "Freud, Einstein—Marshall McLuhan?" *Newsweek* asked in a 1967 cover story on "the McLuhan Explosion."

But McLuhan's conception of the global village was, in an enormous (but limited) sense, quite accurate. Instead of the inward-looking *self*-consciousness bred by the solitary reading of printed matter, the electronic age "brings oral and tribal ear-culture to the literate West," and in turn the Western technology brings the revolution to the whole world, sealing the "entire family into a single global tribe." He's not simply saying that all around the planet we're watching *Dallas*, though that's part of it. He's saying that television changes us—we once again are hearing and seeing our information directly, as if we were talking around a campfire, instead of having it written—translated into arbitrary symbols and given to us to decode. As a result, we will become like preliterate tribesmen of old, except on a much larger scale. As television unites us into a "single consciousness," says McLuhan, we'll turn from our preoccupations with self, which he sees as decadent, to a primitive wholeness.

Assume for a minute that this is true, and lay aside the obvious objection that such a trend is anti-individual, contrary to the path we've followed since ancient Greece. There is, as I've tried to point out, at least an argument to be made for village life, on environmental and cultural grounds. The question is, What aspects of a village can be usefully translated to an almost infinitely larger scale? What is a village? What is a tribe?

When people in villages traditionally got together to talk, they talked about what they had in common. What the weather was like and what it meant for the crops; what the people in the next village were up to and if they meant harm; who in town was causing trouble and who needed help. The talk had real content, and the smaller the village the deeper that content was because everyone could agree on what was important—the talk was rooted in the particular facts of its local existence. By contrast, it obviously makes little sense for the global village to talk about the weather, since while some are harvesting others are planting; we could and should talk about the greenhouse effect or nuclear war, since they're a form of international weather, but we do so only occasionally. And since, as Ted Turner makes clear, one of the pieties of the global village is that there are no other tribes (especially now that the Iron Curtain tribe has given in and switched on CNN, too), there's usually no great threat to discuss. When there is, the limits on our global village become clear—during the war with Iraq, which was portrayed as a moment of great international community, most of the people in the Arab countries and much of the Third World seem to have been repelled by our conduct. Many Americans looked at CNN and swelled with pride at our smart bombs; many people elsewhere looked at CNN and swelled with indignation at the sight of high technology destroying teenage soldiers.

Since we must restrict our conversation to what we have in common, our global-village campfires are not as productive as the old tribal ones. We can find subjects of interest to all only by *erasing* content, paring away information—the things that interest me may not interest, or even be comprehensible, to you. A couple of years ago, for instance, Britain was rife with rumors that McDonald's was sending money to the Irish Republican Army. It turned out that CNN had reported that the hamburger giant had set up individual retirement accounts for its employees. This was a mix-up between two of the nations on earth that have the most in common, including a language—the only solution is to simplify.

You can see this trend away from content almost every time you go the movies. As foreign audiences have grown much larger (and perhaps as America has grown less distinctive), producers and directors have flattened out their films—set them in more ecumenical places, or at least in the most internationally familiar parts of America. "We have to consider the global market, and we absolutely need more universal stories now," a producer told an interviewer recently. "It will be harder to sell a purely American story of an Iowa farmer than something of broader interest." What is of broader interest is Arnold Schwarzenegger, the world's biggest box-office draw and an actor who is not recognizably American. He's an illustration from an anatomy textbook, a set of body parts—one of the few things we share across all borders. And a guaranteed superhuge international smash is something like Arnold Schwarzenegger in *Total Recall*, which takes place in the vicinity of Mars, equidistant from everyone on the planet. Demographics dominate, and content—information—necessarily shrinks.

Which is not to say that McLuhan was wrong. We *do* have a global village, more and more all the time. Its content is one of the few things that can be successfully translated across languages, customs, climates, political tendencies, religions, and the other varied circumstances of people's lives—a certain range of consumer products. This we can all agree on: Levi's are cool. Big Mac. Coke adds life. (Although, according to legend, that particular slogan when translated into one African language reads "Coke brings your ancestors back from the dead.") Marketers are even more interested in McLuhan than academics—as Craig Lambert wrote in a recent issue of *Harvard* magazine, "The global village is here, and its rhythms will grow steadily louder, becoming a backbeat to virtually every aspect of life throughout the 1990s and into the 21st century." He quoted from business school professor Theodore Leavitt's manifesto on "The Globalization of Markets," which cited "the booming success of McDonald's everywhere from the Champs-Elysées to the Ginza, of Coca-Cola in Bahrain and Pepsi in Moscow, and of rock music . . . Hollywood movies, Revlon cosmetics, Sony television, and Levi jeans everywhere." The global corporation, said Leavitt, "looks to the nations of the world not for how they are different but for how they are alike. . . . It seeks constantly in every way to standardize everything into a common global mode."

Along the way, of course, the global village relentlessly roots out the real villages that still remain and drains away their content, their information. Even in the poorest countries advertising is constant. According to a recent article in the magazine *Adbusters*, in the Ivory Coast, "advertising is helping to change the Ivorian attitude toward aging, making women fear looking older and undermining the traditional respect for elders"—which of course represents a significant loss of information because the old people are the wise people, the people who understand the land. And the village fabric is unraveled in other ways. "Traditional drinks are consumed only in social settings, as evidenced by the large pot where they are stored. Yet the advertising of Coca-Cola and Heineken portrays drinking as an individual act rather than a collective one." Instead of the dense and chewy content a local culture develops over many generations to serve its particular survival needs, there is only the sugary-sweet, brightly colored gossamer-light content of the global village—Coke is it.

None of this would have surprised McLuhan—this is not some unexpected hitch in his system. He wrote with huge satisfaction of "an African who took great pains to listen each evening to the BBC News, even though he could understand nothing of it." That is, content mattered not at all—"just to be in the presence of those sounds at 7 P.M. each day was enough for him." And McLuhan anticipated, even celebrated, its commercial use—"since highly skilled and perceptive teams of talent cooperate in the making of an ad for any established line of goods whatever, it is obvious that an acceptable ad is a vigorous dramatization of communal experience. Ads . . . are magnificent accumulations of material about the shared experience and feelings of the entire community." And it's not just ads—the programs that do the best around the world are the ones where appliances star alongside people. When *Dallas* was finally broadcast in Russia in the spring of 1991, a *Wall Street Journal* correspondent watched the first episode with some Muscovites in a crowded apartment. Comparing Texas opulence with Soviet poverty became the evening's running joke, he reported. " 'Look at the gas station,' says Natalia as Bobby Ewing drives his red Mercedes into one. 'Just like ours.'

" 'The cars are, too,' replies her mother, laughing.

" 'How much does a car like that cost in America?' wonders Yuri."

Which is not to say Russians shouldn't want convertibles—if you'd ever driven a Lada you'd want one too. But the fact that the same ad can appeal to someone in a New York apartment and an Iowa farm and an African village does not prove that these situations are alike. It is merely evidence that the people living in them have a few feelings in common, or can be made to have a few feelings in common, and it is these barest, most minimal commonalities that are the content of the global village. The incredibly rich accumulation of lore and practical knowledge and custom, subtly different from each of the millions of villages on earth to the next, erodes in the tide of a few primal pieces of information—this tastes sweet; fashionable people dress like this. The definition of a valuable, working village is a place where it would be very *difficult* for an outsider to fit in because there would be so much to learn, to know, to understand. So many customs, techniques, rituals, orders, stories—*so much information.* The definition of television's global village is just the contrary—it's a place where there's as little variety as possible, where as much information as possible is wiped away to make "communications" easier. The definition of the global village was provided all day in ads for the AT&T Universal Card: "One World, One Card." The global village of which we all speak carelessly is at most a global convenience store.

The mountain says you live in a particular place. Though it's a small area, just a square mile or two, it took me many trips to even start to learn its secrets. Here there are blueberries, and here there are bigger blueberries. The swamp is impenetrable here, but easy to skirt on the other side. You pass a hundred different plants along the trail—I know maybe twenty of them. One could spend a lifetime learning a small range of mountains, and once upon a time people did. But to what end now? A day of television reminds you that except for whatever specialty you earn your living with, you live in a vastly simpler place. A place where your physical location hardly matters. We dwell at the intersection of *Oprah* and *Love Connection,* of *General Hospital* and *You Deserve a Break Today* and *Hawaii Five-O* and *She's the Sheriff,* all of which make as much sense in Seattle as they do in Miami, all of which can be dubbed or copied around the planet and enjoyed by people who inhabit the same general placelessness. All of which can be understood by nineteen-year-olds and ninety-year-olds; all of which can be understood in a matter of seconds by someone who switched them on halfway through. If my endless day of television reminded me of anything, it's that electronic media have become an environment of their own—that to the list of neighborhood and region and continent and planet we must now add television as a place where we live. And the problem is not that it exists—the problem is that it supplants. Its simplicity makes complexity hard to fathom.

So Buckminster Fuller's airborne epiphany, his sense that now he "saw the earth realistically as a sphere," is both a victorious and a bogus idea. If you looked down from your airplane window and saw the momentary mountains and the fleeting fields, and tried very hard to imagine what it would be like to live in each of those places—then you would have some tenuous sense of at least how much information you were missing. Not nearly as strong a sense you would get if you walked to your destination or took a boat, but at least a slight feeling for the magnificent flatness and diversity of the earth. On the last few planes I've flown, though, even this gesture is impossible. The stewards have made everyone pull down the window shades because the sunlight cast a glare on the little film about the duty-free shopping that precedes the Arnold Schwarzenegger movie.

10:00 A.M.

According to CNN, a statue of Philo Farnsworth was unveiled yesterday in the Capitol Rotunda in Washington, D.C. As a sixteen-year-old high school student in Provo, Utah, Philo described to his physics teacher the idea for what he called an "image dissector," or camera tube. Five years later, in 1927, he used the device to transmit a picture—appropriately, a picture of a dollar sign. That's the outside limit on the history of television—at most it's sixty-five (and unlikely to retire). A better date might be 1939, when NBC introduced the first regular television service and FDR became the first president to go on the air, or 1941, when the first commercial transmitters started broadcasting. In truth, though, television as we know it was postponed by World War II, and it wasn't until 1946 or 1947 that people started buying sets in any real numbers. That is to say, television we would recognize stretches back just over forty years. But because of TV's power, and even more its limits, those forty years comprise most of our sense of the world, at least if we were born in the period. We know this time stunningly well—it is a nuanced, subtle familiarity unlike anything else in history.

This is a most curious distortion of our sense of time, as odd as the distortion of space I've just discussed. We don't know the past forty years so well because they just happened—if that were the case we'd have a gradual tailing off in our knowledge, with the seventies much more vivid than the sixties. We know the period because we watch it constantly, over and over. The history—social, cultural, musical, economic, political—of the last forty years appears every day a thousand times on our screens, more and more frequently all the time. There are now a hundred channels airing TV shows—most of them produce at best a few hours a week of their own programming. So they must turn to the shows produced by just three networks for forty years, and show them again and again. You could spend an entire day hopping from channel to channel, never leaving sixties sitcoms. And this is not mere filler. Cable channels like Nickelodeon have discovered large numbers will watch the past head-on against network fare—in a row they run *Dobie Gillis, Bewitched, Green Acres, Donna Reed, Saturday Night Live, Rowan and Martin's Laugh-*

In, My Three Sons, Patty Duke, Make Room for Daddy, then back to *Dobie Gillis.* The networks understand this appeal too—in 1990 they ran a movie called *Gunsmoke: The Last Apache,* as well as *Return to Green Acres,* updates of *Candid Camera, Dark Shadows, Lassie,* and *To Tell the Truth,* and a program called *The Brady Brides.* As *Rolling Stone* noted, it was appropriate that the final episode of CBS's *Newhart* series "ended with Bob waking up in bed with Suzanne Pleshette, his co-star from his seventies vehicle, *The Bob Newhart Show.* Or, as Lisa Kennedy pointed out in the *Village Voice,* on the new Fox network "almost every show refers knowingly to some other point in TV history: 'Totally Hidden Video' to 'Candid Camera,' '21 Jump Street' to 'The Mod Squad,' 'The Simpsons' to the Charlie Brown specials. . . ." Advertisers are hip as well—Coca-Cola has resurrected its classic hilltop commercials, and Mr. Peanut shills once more for Planters. We are happily trapped in a familiar museum, condemned to know in unbelievable detail the attitudes and styles of this one strange period. What happened before, except for a few big Hollywood movies from the sound era, will always seem strange and dreamlike because it isn't on television.

To understand the depth of this absorption, look at the oldest things on television. A whole series of cartoons without main characters date from the forties—they're small, exquisitely animated operas, and they're shown regularly in the preschool and home-from-school slots. They are among the only punctures in this closed system—since there wasn't TV, or just barely, they had to deal with content from before television. There's one of a bookshelf, for instance—Little Women emerge from a cover to swoon over Frank Sinatra. Mother Goose appears, too, and Kim; the wolf from "Little Red Riding Hood" chases Daffy Duck, until a cop steps off the cover of the *Police Gazette* to arrest him; the judge from *Judge* magazine, which ceased publication before the Depression, delivers the verdict, and the wolf falls into Dante's Inferno. On a Merrie Melodies short called *Goofy Groceries,* the cow on the condensed milk croons to the bull on the tobacco case. "Wiggly" gum turns into Little Egypt the stripper, while the navy beans rescue the can-can (tomato) dancers from the Animal Cracker ape. I have no idea what kids make of this—I imagine most of it goes over their heads, as when Porky Pig, in the Foreign Legion, goes off to a Legion convention in Boston to hear an address by General Delivery, or when Popeye goes to the jungle in a faithful Stanley and Livingstone reenactment ("Dr. Bluto, I presume"). The crackle of reference after reference, all from the world before television, many of which go over *my* head, makes these shows sound hypnotically different from the fare just a decade or two later. By then, Wilma is saying to Fred and Betty and Barney, "Let's have our kind of fun tonight. Let's just stay home, curl up in front of the TV, and make some popcorn." Stone Age life is utterly familiar—that's the joke. It's lifted straight from *The Honeymooners.*

TV can't go back before 1900, obviously—to TV that is a black hole that can't be illuminated because there is no film. It's all prehistory, cave paintings, to be explored only occasionally in a costume drama. But since it's a costume drama, it doesn't seem *real,* and we have a deep and intuitive sense of the "real"—real is when you have a picture of it, even if it's a soap opera. A good crisp picture—the newsreel images from the cusp of the TV age look a little off. Did boxers really fall differently when they were punched in the thirties and forties? The herky-jerkiness, the sudden, fast drop to the canvas, make the fight films seem odd, dated, the way that crowds move too fast through the streets in Chaplin films. There must be technical reasons—whatever they are, we instantly recognize these images as outside television, as archival. Even once the camera worked smoothly, it took a while for nonactors to learn to look natural. One documentary on A&E showed newsreel footage of Eisenhower inaugurating the Echo 1 satellite: he spoke at the microphone like someone ordering from the McDonald's drive-through. "It gives me great personal satisfaction to participate in this communications experiment," he said, unconvincingly. JFK appeared in another documentary that day. He was, of course, a vastly different man, but that was only part of it—more important, broadcasting was no longer a historic event. Pausing on his hotel steps to banter with reporters, he grinned his broad grin and said, "I am the man who accompanied Jacqueline Kennedy to Paris." The distance between that moment and the present is as nothing.

And after that, nothing looks "old." Not Fred MacMurray lecturing his boys, not the Dick Van Dyke living room with the famous ottoman. The Mary who lived in that house stood for a very different time than the Mary who worked with Ted and Murray and Lou, but they're both utterly and equally accessible to us—neither looks "off." It's only mild nostalgia that we feel looking at them: it's much more a sense of easy familiarity. They don't clash. Time within the TV period is fluid, usable—we can all deconstruct and reassemble it like a nation of PhD candidates. Consider, for example, a program on the USA network called *Hollywood Insider.* On this night it reported that Carol Burnett was returning to TV after ten years away—it showed a scene from her old show that looked mighty familiar, in part because reruns have kept it continually on the air. Then there was a report on New Kids on the Block mania, complete with swooning girls, followed immediately by a story on the films of the Beatles, including a clip of them running from swooning girls. It's not as if this continuity were hard to see; the hostess of *Hollywood Insider* delivered a commentary that made this very point. "An old TV trend is repeating itself—prime time is getting back to basics," she said. "Back in the fifties and sixties, TV seemed to be in love with the average little guy, the average Joe and Jane. Shows like *The Honeymooners*—average folks in fairly mundane surroundings. Over the years, many would say that TV stars evolved into beautiful people in fabulous surroundings," she said, citing *Dallas* and *Dynasty*. "But now that we're beginning a new decade, it appears we're beginning to turn away from the glitz, back to real families in real situations." There was hardly time for this commentary to sink in before she reported on a new TV movie about the Archie gang after high school. "Now Archie and Veronica are yuppies," the hostess said. "You'll find out what the gang from Riverdale High School is up to now that they're thirtysomething." What Veronica is up to is being a divorcée in a black peignoir. Jughead is a psychoanalyst.

Or consider the strange case of Martha Quinn, who was one of the original veejays a decade ago on MTV. Then she was hip, up-to-the-minute. All the other original veejays have long since been replaced with much younger kids, but Martha is still there, and she's swung back through time. Here she is in a crushed-velvet gown, like something from a chic Haight thrift store. "The other day I heard on the radio—the radio station played the entire album of *Sergeant Pepper's,*" she's saying in her appealing goofy, straight-haired way. "And I was completely blown away: I was thinking, that was back in 1967, and that was when, like, *The Letter* by the Boxtops was out, or Lulu's *To Sir With Love.* Those were the albums that were on the chart. And all of a sudden Paul McCartney's whole concept of Sergeant Pepper's Lonely Hearts Club Band. Absolutely incredibly mind-blowing. And the man who came up with the *concept* of the *idea* of that being a band, Sergeant Pepper's, is coming up." And, sure enough, here came Paul McCartney, equal parts cute Beatle and "serious musician" and venerated star singing his new single.

You don't have to have been there physically to achieve this kind of fluency—the next song, "Put the Message in the Box," was by a group called World Party, whose members looked as if they had been, maybe, in fourth grade when the Jefferson Airplane sang "White Rabbit." And yet they'd painstakingly made their video appear as if it had emerged in, say, May of 1969. There's a guy in a tricornered hat looking as if he's stepped off the cover of a certain

Paul Revere and the Raiders album. A Hindu deity with many arms flashes up on the screen. The lead singer has those big pillowlike headphones around his neck. Wait—the picture is revolving! "See the world in just one grain of sand, You better take a closer look; don't let it slip right through your hand." Oooh. Every detail is right, down to the wide, colorfully embroidered guitar strap. This music was not being sold to forty-year-old nostalgics; it was being sold to kids, who were buying. I was teaching at a program that summer that drew college students from around the country, and half of them arrived in tie-dye. Other hot groups on MTV that day included Wilson Phillips (offspring of Mamas, Papas, and Beach Boys) and Nelson, the sons of rock 'n' roll but especially TV star Ricky Nelson. The *grandsons* of Ozzie and Harriet.

Our sense of time within these television years is so deft that we can make all sorts of jokes from it. One ad features a man from an imaginary organization called the 70s Preservation Society offering an album called *Those Fabulous '70s,* with songs like the Partridge Family's "I Think I Love You," and the Bay City Roller's "S-A-T-U-R-D-A-Y Night," and "The Night Chicago Died," and "Billy, Don't Be a Hero." Time/Life, a sort of cataloguing service for the images of this era, sells a sounds-of-the-seventies set, one volume per year. Or you can buy uncut versions of the great *Beverly Hillbillies* episodes, or expand your *Looney Tunes* Library. This is our cultural patrimony. A Mr. Ira Gallen, the host of a cable program that takes "an affectionate glance at the TV programs of the fifties and sixties," told *The New York Times* recently, "I belong to the first generation able to look back to a blatantly documented childhood. Everything we ate, drank, wore, touched was seen on television and is there for all time." There, every day, at every turn, TV life is being lived in great, exhaustive detail by people who weren't alive when it happened the first time. But the point is, it's still happening.

TV itself is without a doubt the most single important development of the last forty years, and it endlessly refers to itself, which adds to the strange sense you are pickling in its juices. The most fanatic environmentalist doesn't recycle with half the relish of television producers: Turn on HA! the "humor" network that later merged with the Comedy Channel, and you see a *rerun* of *TV's Bloopers and Practical Jokes*—that is, a rerun of a collection of old, old clips introduced by Dick Clark and Ed McMahon, who themselves have been here forever. What funny film they've got! Look—Willard Scott has lost his hairpiece! A newslady gets the date wrong—it's not Monday, it's *Wednesday*! A camera catches a technician crawling off the set! Then they show some "sexy foreign commercials"—"Their regulations are a lot more relaxed," Dick explains as he introduces a reel of salacious Italian ads. It's as if television is some root crop that Indians have learned to use for flour and rope and clothes and poison for the tips of arrows—even the mistakes made on TV are lovingly collected. Advertisements stay as monuments in our minds—on the *Today* show, three jingle writers have appeared to sing their greatest hits, like "Good time, great taste of McDonald's," or "Can't beat the real thing," or "All aboard Amtrak," or "Listen to the heartbeat of America." On *Top Card,* on the Nashville network, contestants need to know if Carly Simon's "Anticipation" was the song for Hunt's or Heinz ketchup, and to recognize the Marlboro theme song, which hasn't been played for two decades, since Congress outlawed televised cigarette commercials. Even when the question's *not* about TV, we assume it must be. On a forgettable program called *Win, Lose, or Draw,* a contestant is trying to illustrate the phrase "Father, Son, and the Holy Ghost," but all the celebrity can think of is "Father Delvecchio," a minor sitcom character nonetheless lodged firmly in millions of minds.

The talk shows, of course, are mostly about TV—turn on something like, say, *Everyday,* with Joan Lunden, and you'll see an interview with MTV's downtown Julie Brown, and a *This Is Your Life* segment reuniting an actor named Tony Cevalier with his high school principal. When a man who holds the world record for squat thrusts appears, it's like a visit from aliens—refreshing aliens from some planet without TV. The news has the same internal preoccupations—all day it reported that Kelsey Grammer (Dr. Crane on *Cheers*) had missed a court-ordered drug rehabilitation date. But there he was on *Cheers,* drinking beer! Nearly every newscast also reported in great detail on the suicide the previous day of a dwarf actor named David Rappaport who had appeared regularly on *L.A. Law.* On *L.A. Law* itself, ruthless Roz resigned from the firm. The show ended, the news came on, and there was Diana Muldaur, the actress who played Roz, giving a long interview about her role. "She horrifies me, to be honest. Every time

I read a script I say, 'Oh no, she's not going to do that. It's just too horrible.' " It was like watching a postgame interview with an athlete, except that Roz was fully clothed.

There're all sorts of comedy on television—whole networks devoted to stand-up routines—and an awful lot of jokes refer to TV, the great common reference. Here's a brilliant impression of *The Six Million Dollar Man!* The theme from *Hawaii Five-O* on a kazoo! There's even one comic on *An Evening at the Improv* whose shtick consists of impersonating a TV switching constantly from one channel to the next. Layers of reference pile upon one another like the ruins of successive cities—to promote its reruns of *Dobie Gillis,* Nickelodeon uses the slogan "Man, it's like Gilligan in a goatee."

In the end, this staggering absorption with TV culture comes at a price. History is weirdly foreshortened—for instance, all anniversaries from the TV period are marked with great care and attention, at least if whatever happened was captured on film. This was the day before the twentieth anniversary of the shooting at Kent State, so everyone was gearing up their coverage—digging out the shaky home movies of the Guardsmen and the students facing one another across the practice field, and the clips of Cronkite delivering the news, and expert after expert agreeing that this incident, seen immediately all across America, "brought the war home." Which is fine—but nothing that comes *before* television is covered in any detail at all. The brightness surrounding the last forty years blinds us to all that preceded it—and forty years is a very short time, even to an individual. Bob Hope, for instance, came on the J. C. Penney shopping channel to hawk his new book. We know Bob Hope from years of specials, from footage of him entertaining the troops. But he is an old man, too. He's talking about World War II, and tells a joke about how FDR trained his dog Fala on the *Chicago Tribune.* The interviewer brays—convulses—but it's hard to believe he has any idea about Colonel McCormick's feud with Roosevelt; Bob might as well tell Saint Thomas Aquinas jokes. The past fills our minds, but only the past of the last four decades. As a result, those four decades seem utterly normative to us, the only conceivable pattern for human life.

But the last forty years have actually been an exceptional period in human history. All the trends I discuss in this book—the retreat from nature, the rapid globalization, the loss of the skills needed for self-sufficiency, and so on—all came to full blossom in this period. It is the most discontinuous, jarring, strange, out-of-the-ordinary stretch of time since we climbed down from trees—a short bender in the more sober course of history. By some estimates, for example, human beings have used more natural resources since the end of World War II than in all the rest of human civilization. This needs to be seen for the binge it is, and it probably needs to end—sooner rather than later, we need sustainable, steady-state societies that live off the planet's interest and not its capital. But if you marinate in the images of the last forty years for hour upon hour and day after day, this binge seems utterly standard, and it's exceedingly hard to even imagine other models, societies, ideas.

There are shows that become part of the oversoul—

take *The Brady Bunch,* whose theme song is as widely known as the national anthem, whose example is invoked over and over. A Showtime program on divorce, for instance, shows a bewildered kid saying, "We were like a very hip *Brady Bunch.*" In Chicago and now New York, standing-room crowds jam a theater each week to see a different *Brady Bunch* episode performed live. The Lifetime network, on one of its talk shows, convened a summit of sitcom moms. All sorts of women were there—the mom from *One Day at a Time,* and the woman that Fred MacMurray finally married for the last season of *My Three Sons,* and Mrs. Jefferson, and Molly Dodd's mother, and even the actress who played Mrs. Munster. But they all deferred to Florence Henderson, Mrs. Brady, who talked about how every parent strives for a union like that between the Bradys, and said that psychiatrists used tapes of the show when counseling couples. (A job that may have grown more interesting after the recent revelation, on *Geraldo,* of course, that the actor playing eldest son Greg had dated Ms. Henderson during the filming of the show.) A recent survey of twenty-one- to twenty-five-year-olds commissioned by MTV revealed that their favorite program was *The Brady Bunch,* which ended its original run when they were three- to seven-year-olds. "I think it gave people hope that there was a family like that," Mrs. Brady said. An utterly *normal* family—their "gimmick" was *not* being a rock band or an interracial mix or robots. Ostensibly they were two separate families, four guys and four gals ("with hair of gold like their mother's"), that had come together. But this never caused any tension in the show. Almost nothing ever caused tension—it was just kids being kids and parents being parents.

A professor from the State University of New York told the Lifetime audience: "My students know the Brady Bunch better than their own parents' birth dates." That is, they know a life where no work is done, usually not even by the maid, because there are appliances in every corner. They know a life where everything happens in a big and isolated suburban home. Where parents are mostly pals, where money flows in, where food appears. We can make fun of it, laugh at it, but all of us who grew up with it (which means nearly everyone born since it went on the air) are affected by it. Very few of us can afford to live like the Bradys—even the *hope* of such a life-style, which once seemed the obvious promise of the future, is fading as the middle class shrinks, as even a child or two require both parents to work. And even if individuals can afford it, it's also become clear that the planet probably can't—that the world, were it composed of a billion Brady Bunches, would buckle under the environmental strain. We may recognize, almost instinctively, these problems. The absurd excess of the eighties, the painful slowdown of the nineties—many of us are left wondering if there isn't some other path. But *The Brady Bunch* and all its imitators are what we know in our hearts. And so the search for something different—something more sustainable and maybe less sterile—never gets under way. Because we *know* what normal is.

Noonday

Unable though I was to forecast the weather, I retained sufficient mother wit to recognize that it had turned into a gorgeous day, and so I set out to climb Blackberry Mountain, Crow's smaller neighbor.

From the pond I followed a brook down to the valley between the peaks—it is a mossy cool trickle in the summer, and instead of clambering over deadfall along the banks you can hop easily from rock to rock down the creek. I stopped occasionally at the small clear pools to admire the water striders, their legs dimpling the tense surface, their small bodies casting impressive shadows on the creek bottom as they went about their inscrutable business.

When I reached the valley between the mountains, I could look up at the open cliffs at the top of Blackberry. Since there's no trail to the summit, I just hit out along a compass bearing through the woods. The bottom slopes have been logged in the last couple of decades—the sun pours into the clearings, which of course are luxuriant with thorny berry cane. I fought my way through, and after twenty minutes or so, as the slope steepened, rock patches began to appear—the trees were fewer and bigger, and in the shade of one hemlock I lay down to rest. After about ten minutes, at least a dozen small birds began to resume the activity I had interrupted with my noisy arrival. They were mostly small thrushes, and they flew in and out of the branches in what looked like a high-speed game of tag, over and over, lighting now on a swaying bough, then launching themselves off into the air once more.

After my rest I climbed the remaining distance to Blackberry's long summit ridge, and walked out along the top of the steep cliffs that faced back to Crow. The wind was blowing below—I could hear it rush like white water and see where it was riffling the maple tops in the mountain valley—but up on top it was still, and the sun baked the fragrant pine needles. I was sitting, drinking from my canteen, when I saw a vulture appear way below in the draw between the mountains. He circled slowly and methodically up, holding his wings in a stiff, lacquered bow, never flapping, always soaring. Eventually, after perhaps a half hour, he was directly above me on the cliffs, perhaps a hundred feet in the air, still circling. He was joined there by four, then five, finally six others, circling so close I could count feathers. When they passed directly overhead it was nearly unbearable—almost erotic—this feeling of being watched. At moments I felt small and vulnerable, like prey; if they disappeared from view for a minute I wanted to know where they were. But by the time I finally rose to go back to my tent on Crow, I felt almost protected, watched over. It had been thrilling—my heart was beating hard.

Still and all, by the standards of television nature, the water striders and the thrushes and even the vultures were hardly worth mentioning. I had not been gored, chased, or even roared at. I had failed to tranquilize anything with a dart; no creature had inflated stupendous air sacs in a curious and ancient mating ritual, or eaten its young, or done any of the other prodigious tricks that happen around the clock on nature television. You could spend nearly the whole day watching nothing but nature documentaries, and if you did you would emerge exhausted. Nature on TV is the job of a man named Graham or Ian or Nigel who makes every announcement ("Using his incisors like a comb, the marmot attends to his thick underfleece") sound like Churchill in wartime. The point of the show can be that, say, elephants are all but exterminated in a certain African refuge, but you can be sure that our host will find one. Not one—dozens. "I think there's a jolly good chance of sketching this lot," the host is saying as he piles out of his Land-Rover. "There's the matriarch—she's the one to watch. I'd be crazy to get too close to her. If I can reach that anthill I can get some good sketches. She's accompanied by uncles and aunties of all ages—the young males get kicked out because they get stroppy." On the voiceover, the narrator may be confessing the boring truth: "Lions are lazy—the males are the worst. They'll sleep twenty hours a day if they get the chance." But on the screen the lions are training their young by chasing jackals and other exotic game—Oooh, so much for that zebra. The man in the jeep, obligatory spare tire on the hood, tracks the lion pack toward a watering hole, never losing sight of them. He spies some ostriches: "Ostriches mean water, and water means life—and the lion feels an ancient urge. Perhaps she's come upon a place to start a pride." Oooh—lion sex! Cubs come tumbling out after a two- or three-minute gestation, full of play, and the timeless predatory cycle repeats—Oooh, poor wildebeest. Switch the channel and someone is releasing a seal from a California aquarium. He starts to travel north, but suddenly a killer whale is on his tail. A brief respite in a kelp bed ("It's the life of Riley, lying on your back and eating crab so fresh it tries to walk away") and then our seal resumes his trip up the coast to the Pribilofs, where the breeding beach is a great heaving mass of flippers. At the precise moment our hero washes ashore, the men appear with the baseball bats for the annual fur harvest; fortunately he retreats to the safety of the ocean before they can get him, still alive for the documentaries that will surely follow.

It would be churlish to complain about these gorgeous films. It would be even more churlish to quote from a recent interview in *Entertainment Weekly* with Wolfgang Bayer. An acclaimed nature photographer who's made dozens of TV films, he tells of hoisting tame, declawed jaguars into trees for action scenes, and spray-painting pet-shop ferrets till they're ringers for the nearly extinct black-footed variety, and starving piranhas so they'll attack with more ferocity. He once did a show on an Amazonian tarantula that occasionally eats birds. How often does it eat birds, asked the reporter? "As often as as you throw them to him," he says. It would be churlish because TV nature films have without any question done an immense amount of good—species exist today that would be fossil records if Philo Farnsworth hadn't invented the picture tube. Your can of tuna has a little "dolphin-safe" symbol on it because in 1963 Chuck Connors starred in a film called *Flipper*, which gave birth to a TV show of the same name. The movie version was shown on May 3—in the month of May alone it was on the Disney Channel five times and on Cinemax twice, so presumably each new generation sees the boy battle his stern, old-fashioned father, who actually believes dolphins are a threat to his fishery. "If they come, we'll kill them. We have no choice," the father says. The rise of environmental consciousness over the intervening three decades can be felt in just how shocking this attitude now seems. Some fishermen still kill dolphins, but they try to hide their work because nearly everyone agrees it is a sick waste; in 1963, obviously, *not* killing dolphins was regarded as revolutionary, and *Flipper* is a key reason for the change.

In 1963, too, the sperm-whale kill reached its peak,

claiming about thirty thousand of the great beasts. We think of whaling as being at its height in the last century, when Nantucket men and Gloucester men and Mystic men and the men of a dozen other ports that are now pricy tourist attractions sailed the globe in search of lamp oil. But the slaughter continued, except of those species that were already reduced below commercial levels, until about the time that a slight Frenchman took to the TV screens. On any given time that day you can see Jacques Cousteau, the John Muir of the deep, two or three times—here he is in the sea grass beds of Australia, a safe pasture for sea cows now threatened by sand-mining; here he is working to "cweate a weef, shimmawing with life." His son Michel is apparently taking over the family trade, and has perfected the sad Gallic intonations of his dad. He is swimming next to a giant grouper—"I hardly ever see a fish so large anymore, which were my constant companions when I began diving. I cannot resist reaching out to this veteran of living, as if to touch the past, the time when big fish were nothing more than that." Cousteau's success can be measured in the sea, where remnant populations of some species survive because of great human efforts, and even more in the popular mind—a four-year-old boy just spent the weekend with us, and his conversation rarely strayed from the topic of killer whales, a species that until quite recently stirred loathing and not love.

Still, measured in the largest terms, such appeals aren't working. That is, virtually everyone in the industrialized world has a television and has presumably, if only by accident, seen many hours of gorgeous nature films—seen a more diverse and wondrous natural world than man could ever have seen before. And yet we're still not willing to do anything very drastic to save that world. We'll buy dolphin-safe tuna if it doesn't cost much extra, but we won't cut back on driving and consuming electricity and doing the other things that lead to global warming, even though the world now loses as much as 5 percent of its coral reefs annually due to higher water temperatures likely caused by the greenhouse effect. Species continue to disappear, and at an accelerating rate; presidents continue to propose, say, drilling for oil in the Arctic National Wildlife Refuge, square in the middle of an enormous caribou herd. Why can't Graham and Ian and Nigel stop this?

They can't, I think, because for all their dart guns and millions of feet of film they actually get across remarkably little information—much less than you'd acquire almost unconsciously from a good long hike. Half the time they specialize in misinformation, undercutting their message with their pictures. The Englishman is telling you that this great flightless bird is on the edge of extinction, but for half an hour he is showing you endless pictures of this great flightless bird, so how bad could it be? The actual numbers of surviving big mammals are astoundingly small—grizzly bears in the lower forty-eight states can be counted in the hundreds. In fact, you've probably seen a large fraction of them at one time or another, wandering slowly through the telephoto field of a Yellowstone camera. But they appear so often they seem numerous. No one shows film of the weeks in camp waiting for the damned gorillas to appear—a documentary of trees that used to be inhabited by the ancient manlike primates but no longer are is a documentary people wouldn't watch, though that void is the true revelation about an awful lot of the world.

Something even more insidious happens when you get most of your nature through television, though—the "real" nature around you, even when it's intact, begins to seem dull. Mr. Bayer, the man with the spray-painted ferrets, said, "If we showed viewers only natural, unadulterated filmmaking, wildlife filmmakers would be out of business in a year, it'd be so boring." So, instead, nature films are like the highlight clips they show on the evening sportscast, all rim-bending slam dunks and bleachers-clearing home runs and knee-crumpling knockout punches. If you'd been raised on a steady diet of such footage and then you went to a game, you'd feel cheated—what is all this business with singles and pop flies? Why do the hockey players skate around for so long between fights? The highlights films erode appreciation for the various beauties of the game, some of which are small and patient.

The problem is even more severe with the natural world, where the ratio of observable high drama is much lower. A movie like *Benji the Hunted,* which was on the Disney Channel, presents the forest as a place where, in the space of a day, you encounter and must vanquish mountain lions, wolves, grizzlies, badgers, and so on right down Noah's list—it is a car-chase flick with animals. (And as impossible in its outcome as most car chases—Benji, a domesticated dog, has somehow retained the instinct necessary to outwit every predatory mammal of the North American continent, while acquiring a remarkably un-

Darwinian compassion for the young of other species.) How disappointing, then, to go for a walk in a healthy Eastern woods and see so few bared claws. In many years hiking in the East I've happened across bears twice. Once, in Maine, I rounded a corner in a trail and there, three feet away, as lost in thought as I had been, sat a black bear. One look at me and she dived for the bushes—total contact time perhaps four seconds. A few years later, walking near my house with my wife, I heard a noise in a treetop and all of a sudden another black bear, roughly the size and shape of a large sofa, dropped to the ground a few yards away. She glowered in our direction and then lit out the opposite way. Time of engagement: maybe seven seconds. Those were grand encounters, and they've spiced every other day I've spent in the woods—on the way up Blackberry Mountain, for instance, I sang as I waded through the berry bushes, aware that this is where any bear with a stomach would be. But if I counted as dramatic only those days when I actually saw a big fierce mammal, I would think the forest a boring place indeed.

Big animals are fairly scarce in the best of conditions, and understandably shy—an Adirondack hunter last fall shot a bear that biologists, studying his teeth, determined was forty-three years old. That is, he'd been hiding out up here since before Truman beat Dewey. When you do see large animals it's usually at a pretty good distance, not right up close as on TV—you can rarely sneak up on, say, a heron the way you can with a zoom lens. (On the other hand, you need a big, natural field of vision to get a sense of the graceful spookiness with which they glide.) But even if you did see a rare animal, and somehow managed to creep up real close, chances are it wouldn't be doing anything all that amazing. Chances are it would be lying in the sun, or perhaps grooming itself, or maybe, like the duck on the pond, swimming back and forth. A lot of animals are remarkably good at sitting still (especially when they suspect they're under surveillance), and this is something TV never captures. The nature documentaries are as absurdly action-packed as the soap operas, where a life's worth of divorce, adultery, and sudden death are crammed into a week's worth of watching—trying to understand "nature" from watching *Wild Kingdom* is as tough as trying to understand "life" from watching *Dynasty*.

This is particularly true because, even at its best, TV covers only a small slice of the natural world. There are perhaps ten million (some say thirty million) species on earth; of those that we know about and have catalogued, only a few meet the requirements for extensive television coverage—cuteness (or grotesqueness so complete it borders on the cute), great amiability or ferocity, accessibility (it lives on grassland plains or beaches, not in the deep ocean, badly lit caves, or rain-forest canopies), correct size to show up well on camera, and so on. Species with these characteristics seem to exist in roughly the same ratio as human television actors to the general population, and they are as consistently overexposed. But even the most unengaging, hard-to-get-at, drab little animal has a great advantage over any plant except a Venus's-flytrap, and that is mobility. In its immense fear that we might grow bored, TV has not yet acquired the courage necessary to show an unmoving picture for very long, and so the only hope of star-struck vegetation is time-lapse photography, which works okay for orchids but doesn't do much for, say, evergreens. Someone sent me a "working treatment" recently for a television program celebrating trees that is being made by a leading wildlife filmmaker. The "tease opening" features "intercutting of striking tree images with interview characters expressing

Wonder
Concern
Reverence

followed by opening credits over breathtaking images of trees and forests" against an "*engaging mix of forest sounds, rain, and music.*" The film covers rain forest, swamps, and the autumn blaze of color; it looks at furniture and at musical instruments made from wood; it covers bonsai and the Yellowstone fires, all in forty-seven and a half minutes, leaving twelve and a half for commercials. Beautiful, no doubt, but perhaps the wrong way to nurture appreciation for trees, whose most glorious characteristic is that they stay in the same place forever. Any time spent in a real forest gives you this information: a tree is of a piece with the soil from which it grows and the sky it rises into, part and parcel of the insect that eats at its middle and the bird that eats the insect, inseparable from the forest of other trees and yet perfect in its humped and gnarly isolation. And yet this is so hard to show—much easier to flash a sequoia on the screen and say this counts because it's big.

The upshot of a nature education by television is a deep fondness for certain species and a deep lack of understanding of systems, or of the policies that destroy those systems. For instance, one of the ads that may come on during this celebration of trees, as it did several times on May 3, is paid for by the Forest Products Council. "Today we have more trees than we did back in 1920," it says, "thanks in part to something our forest products companies do three million times a day—plant a tree." The visuals accompanying this reassuring voice are stunning—from the air we see a bend in a wilderness river with a rich and exuberant old forest spilling forth to the bank. There's a lot less of this kind of forest than there was in 1920, thanks in part (in whole, really) to something else the forest products companies do every day, which is cut down virgin stands of climax forest, the biologically diverse, marvelously complex ancient forest that covered much of this country when Europeans arrived. The forest products companies *do* plant trees. They plant them in nice straight rows, every sapling the same age and the same height and the same species, and then they drop herbicides from helicopters to keep down undesirable varieties; they create, in other words, sterile plantations for growing timber and pulp. And the forest products companies often perform this public service on public lands, under the guidance of government employees. The great national forests, which cover so much of the western part of the nation, are mostly managed as timber farms; the trees, in many cases old-growth forest, are sold to lumber companies and then cut down. One of these public servants is Smokey Bear, whose commercials run all day and night. We all grew up believing Smokey hated forest fires because they fried Bambi's kin, but the truth is Smokey doesn't want you to burn the forest down because his employer, the Forest Service, wants to cut it down instead. You don't see this when you drive through a national forest, because the government employs an enormous corps of landscape architects whose whole job is to make sure the clear-cuts are invisible. And you don't see it on TV because it's political, and a tree is a tree, and it's time to look at the fur seals again.

In 1990, according to *The New York Times,* the "not-to-be-lived-without accessory" was the "personal meadow, a mini-expanse of green grass growing ever-so-sweetly out of a gently rusticated plywood box." "They couldn't walk by without coming in to touch it," said one florist. "It's such a fresh look. People have very strong reactions to it." An interior designer who changes the sod in his foyer every two weeks when it begins to yellow says, "I see it as Eastern in its concept."

Like urban living, TV cuts us off from context—stops us from understanding plants and animals as parts of systems, from grounding them in ideas larger than "fresh" or fierce or cute. And so we don't know what to make of them. We are still pulled toward this natural world, with a tug so strong it must be primal, but TV helps turn it into a zoo; hence most of our responses are artificial. Animals amble across the screen all day and night—I saw the same squad of marching flamingos twice during the day on different networks. ("They're stupid," said the handler on one of the programs. "It took me six months to get them to walk in formation.") CNN, in just a few hours, reported on a new virus that was spreading among macaws, parrots, and cockatoos; an orphanage that had been established for African elephants whose mothers had been killed by poachers; a group of manatees in the waterways of Florida who were being gouged by outboard propellers; a white tiger being born in a zoo; some home videos of dolphins dying in the tuna nets that a man had risked his life to take; a debate about whether people should be permitted to swim in tanks with dolphins; some "doomsday dolphins" that might be trained for ordnance work; and a Navy plan to kill thirty-five thousand feral goats on San Clemente island. The day's main animal feature was a constantly repeated story on the abuses of puppy breeders, a story that also appeared on virtually every network's broadcast. The Humane Society had issued a report that morning—most pet store dogs, it turns out, come from breeders in six Midwestern states, who in many cases raise them in such horrid conditions that they sicken and die after purchase. Two big dogs and their owner came on the *Today* show to chat with Bryant Gumbel about the problem; other networks aired film of puppies crowded together in wire cages. "Her ear canal has been inflamed so long there's no longer any hole in there," said one vet. "Her skin is dry, cracking, bleeding in spots. Boy—I can imagine how uncomfortable she is."

We all can. That's the marvelous thing about pets—our visceral and natural affection for them offers an easy door for human minds to enter into a larger than normal world, a world where our preoccupations count for less. A dog or a cat or a rabbit is a constant reminder that there is more than us out there—our love for them is a healthy recognition of that more. But when that love lacks a larger context, the relationship turns mawkish. Everyone knows about pet cemeteries, but CNN carried the story of a cemetery where people could be buried *with* their pets. The Fox affiliate offered news of a New York company that will freeze-dry your dead pet so you can keep him in your living room. A twenty-pound dog will run you $1,200—"We charge by the pound, but on birds we've got a flat price"—and take four months to prepare. "After we got him back, we'd just put him in his normal position, and people would walk up to him, pet him, joke with him, and then notice he was dead," said one satisfied owner. "Archie was our whole life. Everything we did was for Archie. . . . Even though he wasn't going to be living, we could still stroke him, still tell him how much we loved him."

The healthier relationships always had some content to them—one of the local channels, for instance, carried a fine report about the members of the Fairfax County police K-9 squad, German shepherds who live at the homes of their handlers. "You get very used to grabbing the dog and loving him up," said one cop. But it's a relationship based more on respect—on an appreciation of a dog's nature, his gifts—than on sentiment. "When he gets in the cruiser his personality changes. You can actually see the transition. He has a little dance he does—a twirl like 'Let's get rolling.' " One of the German shepherds, Jake, was stabbed seven times but kept on going—he collared the criminal despite his fatal wounds. "They become such a part of you—it's like losing an arm or a leg or a baby," said his distraught handler. But there was no suggestion that Jake should be freeze-dried—he was too real for that.

In somewhat the same way, the men on a few of the angling programs showed some real connection with their catch—they were both competitors and, in a strange sense, colleagues. "This fish is exhausted beyond any of our beliefs, it's fought so hard," said one hip-booted host of *Fish'n Canada.* "It's your duty as an angler to wait till she's fully revived before releasing her." Don Meissner, the host of *Rod'n'Reel* Streamside, caught a big old brookie: "I tell you, my heart's just a poundin'. Holy cow, oh, oh, holy cow, look at that fish. . . . Since I got older, my feelings on fishing have changed tremendously. It's just to be out there. Not to kill something. Oh my—I'm shaking like a leaf." Now, you could argue that there's something perverse about catching a fish and letting him go, and you could argue that if people really *admired* a fish they wouldn't stick a barb through its lip and pull on it for a quarter of an hour. And if you argued any of those things you might be right. Still, there is an echo of something here, of the traditional respectful relationship between hunters and their quarry.

Even in the most civilized, that tug remains. A Cousteau special on the Turner Broadcasting System showed crowds of Australians climbing off buses to wade along a beach where dolphins lolled in the surf. Some of the people were painfully stupid—sticking their fingers down the dolphin's blowhole. But most seemed genuinely filled with

Wonder
Concern
Reverence

"In ze welcome of ze dolphins lies ze test of human wisdom," said Cousteau, right as usual. Do we appreciate dolphins for the tricks they can perform, for being like limited humans?—the trainer at a Hawaii dolphin show said that she knew her charge was "smart" because "he wants something for nothing." Do we appreciate them as an economic and recreational "resource," like the striped bass described by a hatchery director on *Virginia Wildlife*? (Captured fish are weighed to determine how much hormone, collected from the pituitaries of pregnant women, to inject them with—"Fish in captivity tend to hold back on their eggs, but this overrides that.") Or do we begin to understand again what once was common knowledge—that they're marvelous for their own reasons, that they matter independently of us?

That piece of information can come only when you accept nature and its component parts on their own terms—small and placid and dull and parts of systems, as well as big and flashy and fierce and soulful. Alone on a mountain you do start slowly to learn this lesson—it's inevitable if you lie on your back for hours and watch the hawks just circle, or lie on your stomach and watch the ducks just swim. They are not there for you—they are there because the world belongs to them too. Learn this lesson too well and you are in trouble, for in our current world it will mostly bring pain, mostly breed hysteria. Even on television this pain occasionally surfaces. HBO was showing Diane Fossey's story, *Gorillas in the Mist*—it is the story of a kook, driven mad by her understanding of what was happening around her. On paper her actions look insane—she kidnaps poachers, imprisons them. But watching the gorillas, tugged by that old tug, you know why she did what she did. The gorillas so clearly *belong.* An even better film, and more remarkable considering it was made way back in 1958, is John Huston's *The Roots of Heaven,* an elephant story starring Errol Flynn that aired on the American Movie Channel. "Anyone who's seen the great herds on the march across the last free spaces knows it is something the world can't afford to lose," says the Flynn character, and of course he is right.

But the world *is* losing them—CNN is filled with the pictures of dying elephants and of a dozen other creatures. This is perhaps the ultimate loss of information—too sophisticated to burn books, we burn the planet. Each day information leaks away—some branch of life that evolved for millions of years is gone, and the next day two more, and six the day after that. The world grows stupider, less substantial. And those of us who would fight have little ground on which to stand, for the tug at our hearts from the sad picture on the screen is no substitute for the deep and lifelong understandings we've let slip away.

2:00 P.M.

For the fourth or fifth time today, another channel is showing Robert Tilton's *Success 'n' Life*, "America's personal growth and achievement program." So for the fourth or fifth time today Mr. Tilton is speaking in tongues—it's an unnerving sight because when he speaks in tongues his soothing, sugary voice doesn't change, nor does his puppyish demeanor. "There's a person there with a spot on his lung," he'll say. "Pas o kea camba asaya. Offer unto God thy thanksgiving and ka basota pay thy vows unto the most high." It is as if your waiter said, "Hi, my name is Bob, our special tonight konwa geo mububuy is a tuna steak, that's done in a herb-lemon butter." Tilton, who looks and sounds like a combination of Mister Rogers and the Joker, gets "words of knowledge" from God about viewers with particular frailties. "There's someone with a kidney infection that has spread to other unusual organs," he will announce. The sick are instructed to put their hands on the screen, a practice he insists works as well when the show's on tape as when it's live. He's giggling a little—"I feel in such a happy mood. You see, my emotions are controlled and directed by the spirit of God."

Of all the questions that people have wondered about over the centuries, "What's for dinner?" probably tops the list. But close behind are the questions about God—Is there one? (Or more than one?) What is he or she like? What is my relationship to him or her? Answers to these questions—or at least clues toward answers—are stunningly abundant on both the mountaintop and the TV. Abundant, and utterly different.

On TV— But everyone knows about the TV preachers. They are greedy hypocrites. They get volume discounts at hot-sheet hotels. They rob their flocks and they cheat the IRS. They are unctuous and self-righteous, oozing greenish smarm the way decent folks sweat. They are too well coiffed and wear too much makeup. Years ago, when I was a very young reporter and before Jim and Tammy were really famous, I went down to see the PTL Club in Charlotte, North Carolina, and I can testify firsthand to most of that list of sins. The two of them sat in offices atop a sort of crystal early-Hyatt ziggurat; in the basement of the building, women in long rows slit envelopes and shook out the checks that supported this opulence. In the control room of the TV show, the producers spoke with awe of Tammy's ability to cry on command—a command they gave frequently. And then, on my last night there, something interesting happened. I was stony broke, with only a Shell credit card to get me home to Massachusetts. Before I drove off I went to the nightly church service at the newly opened Heritage USA theme park. The service was as manipulative as usual, but as we were filing out, an old woman appeared at my side clutching a five-dollar bill. "God told me to give you this," she said, and disappeared. I have no certain idea what the point of this story is—not, certainly, that Jim Bakker should be let out of prison. Maybe that the cupidity of the preacher didn't necessarily poison all who watched—that real people with decent hopes were drawn to these messages. Ever since, as I've watched the TV preachers, I've tried not to be distracted by their appetites for the seven major sin groups. I've tried not to be distracted by them at all—tried instead to attend to their message, to the particular vision they send forth of God, and the information it contains.

Above all else, they depict a strangely puny God. He can be easily persuaded to grant human wishes—a sort of genie-in-the-bottle God. Tilton, for instance, refers ceaselessly to a passage in the New Testament about how "if two agree it shall be done." To this end, he has a phone bank full of agree-ers—you call them up and they agree with you about what they want. Luckily for Tilton, there are also some other passages that indicate sending in contributions will help guarantee results. "Your gift will be returned to you in full," Tilton says, quoting Isaiah, or perhaps it'll be returned "a hundredfold." In any event, Robert Tilton has apparently been accredited as an official depository because that's where you're supposed to send the check. You don't need to do it all at once—you can *pledge* a thousand dollars and pay it off fifty dollars per month. Here's a videotape of a woman who made just her first payment in the hope her husband would return—and sure enough he did. And a woman who sent in $33.12 in "seed money," and immediately got a job and now she's making sales "supernaturally." "I sayeth the Lord has the power to make you rich," Tilton proclaims—and indeed *you* have the power to make the Lord make you rich, simply by sending in money. "God told me—those that bless you, I'm going to bless them," Tilton declares.

God has been talking to Larry Lea, too—Larry Lea has raised 251,000 members of a projected 300,000-strong prayer army. His tapes run to fifty dollars, but "God spoke to me, and said whatever you sowed in my ministry he'll return to you in money." (TV Christians invariably "sow" money, even though most of them long since stopped sowing grain.) Morris Cerullo, the California pastor who recently purchased Heritage USA (and who counts home-run champion Darryl Strawberry among his converts), relies on a set of Old Testament passages, the Abrahamic covenants. God promised Abraham a great reward if he and his family were circumcised; through a process called "Abrahamic transference," says Cerullo, this promise now extends to all of us, even if we haven't actually been circumcised, because some later passages from Galatians prove that true circumcision is of the heart. Anyway, it's all worked out in great detail, and then an enormous crowd stands up and sings a jaunty song called "We Are the Circumcision," and an announcer reminds us of the Billion Soul Crusade in the Decade of Destiny and thanks us for remembering that the phone lines are for people with credit cards only, and tells of a vision Morris Cerullo recently enjoyed in which "a blank check appeared over the heads of God's people. But what was so unusual was that it was signed by Jesus Christ himself . . . in order to provide for the financial needs of people." In case anyone was thinking of this as a metaphor, Cerullo produces a huge facsimile of the check, which is drawn on the Bank of Heaven.

It is not surprising that preachers would say such things—the only difference between this and selling indulgences in the fashion of medieval priests is that you no longer need to wait till purgatory to collect. What's interesting is that people would continue to buy it (that they'd literally buy it, in fact). Hope is a powerful force, but still this is a pretty unlikely God, bound by a series of remarks to do the bidding of anyone with a checkbook. He's the automatic teller of deities—and he seems to be ascendant currently over the more traditional vengeful God of the New Right who is so concerned with the short list of sins. Jerry Falwell is still on TV, but the Moral Majority has disbanded and his sermons lack vigor. He's raising money to open the first Christian day-care center in Romania, and he's shouting that Earth Day was created by "the New Age religion," and he's decrying the porn menace, but he's also deeply involved in *very* fine points of doctrine ("I believe in the premillennial, pretribulational coming of Christ for all his church. I don't believe in a mid-trib rapture, a post-trib rapture"). The prosperity theology of preachers like Tilton or Cerullo is, he says, "a bunch of malarkey," but you can almost feel people switching the dial to watch them make their vast promises. The religious channels still carry tirades against atheists (Madalyn Mays O'Hair's followers are supposedly trying to force the removal of an underwater statue of Jesus from a Florida reef owned by the federal government), and homosexuals and rock 'n' roll lyricists and Gus Hall of the Communist Party USA, but it's all wearing a little thin—one show features Nicky Cruz, the gang leader converted in the 1972 Christian classic *The Cross and the Switchblade.* He now appears to be at least fifty (and what an innocent idea a *switchblade* is), and he is inveighing against Ouija boards, which among other things are made by Parker Brothers in Salem, Massachusetts, hotbed of colonial Satanism. Everywhere this God of thwarted desire is giving way to the God who has to work miracles for you—on the *Gospel Bill* show, which is for children, a puppet named Nicodemus is working and working to try to raise some money. Finally his friends convince him he should stop working and start praying—when he does, a hundred-dollar bill arrives in the mail.

Such thinking is not confined to the religious channels—there's a special two-hour episode of *Little House on the Prairie* where one of the boys is shot and seems to be dying a lingering, inevitable death. Pa goes a lot crazy—at least that is what Ma and the preacher and the doctor and the handyman all think. He goes off with the boy for months to a remote meadow, where he builds an altar and prays without cease. And what happens? Do his family and friends slowly win him back to normality, their love easing his deep pain? Does he come to see that God's plan is mysterious, inscrutable to humans? No—on network TV an angel appears, lightning strikes the altar, the boy is healed, and Michael Landon is able to go on to his next series, *Highway to Heaven,* where this time he gets to play the angel and set things right with his supernatural powers. This *Little House* episode is not metaphor—this is NBC insisting that angels come down and heal children if their loved ones offer sufficient prayers.

More conventional Christianity gets much shorter shrift. There's a priest from an inner-city parish, Father Dowling, who appears on ABC, but he interests the network only for his ability to deduce the murderer of a prostitute—he tracks down the cop gone bad, but doesn't even get to deliver a homily about it. And then there's ACTS, one of the six religious channels. It is sponsored by the old-line Protestant denominations, the eminently reasonable Congregationalists and Presbyterians and such. It shows one solid, somewhat dull program after another, most of which chronicle the good works that various church agencies perform. The Methodists showed how they help youthful offenders in the Midwest make restitution for their crimes instead of going to prison; the Lutherans staged a drama about a young black preacher who had gone to work lobbying for hunger relief on Capitol Hill. These programs strike me as sound—I'm a Methodist myself. Their emphasis on giving instead of getting accurately reflects the demands of a tough and radical gospel. The good-hearted and faithful people appearing on this network do a good job of describing how we should behave in *response* to God. But something is missing here too—a sense of the *experience* of God, of the presence of the sacred that led people and societies to religion in the first place. And one reason this sense is lacking, even in the most selfless of these programs, is that their God seems to have an absorbing, almost obsessive interest in our species, our societies, our problems. He is first and foremost a god of history—of the human story alone. He is not *controlled* by human beings the way that Tilton's magic God is, but he seems shrunken nonetheless—muffled, captive.

The mountaintop offers different information—there some grand order seems both manifest and enormous, far larger than the purely human world. History, too, shows a profoundly different idea about the divine. "As a species, humans do know God," writes Erazim Kohak, a philosopher at Boston University and the author of a remarkable book, *The Embers and the Stars.* Kohak points out that anthropologists use the evidence of worship as a key way to distinguish between humans and higher primates. It is only with distance from the natural, larger world that this recognition begins to dim—in ancient forests, he says, there are no atheists. "Of all the illusions of the world of artifacts and constructs, the most facile and most palpably false is the claim that the awareness of God's presence—in our inept phrase 'believing in God'—is the preaching of certain individuals, an opinion contingently held by some members of the species. The obverse is true. It is the blindness to God's presence that is exceptional. Humans, as a species, throughout the millennia and all over the globe, have been worshippers of the Holy. The awareness of God's presence is and ever has been the most persistent specific trait of our species."

Very little of this unbounded pre-Christian religion appears on television. (There was a woman who claimed to practice the ancient and fascinating goddess religion; unfortunately, this particular priestess was under indictment because she had taken "sacrificial offerings" in return for sex. "I've had vaginal intercourse with two thousand six hundred and eighty-five men," she declared cheerfully to a crowd of reporters who stood giggling like schoolboys on the courthouse steps.) Most days, in fact, no one gives voice to this feeling for the divine that predates Moses and Christ—the sense that the world is a sacred place usually goes unmentioned in the nature documentaries or the religious programs. Not because it is extinct—there are rather a lot of us, I suspect, who still feel closest to God in the woods or on a beach staring out at the waves. But such feelings don't lend themselves to organization or to commerce, and so they are normally silent.

This day, however, something unusual was going on—a Hawaiian volcano called Kilauea was erupting and burying the small town of Kalapana in a blanket of lava. Since it was otherwise a slow news day, Ted Koppel spent a fascinating *Nightline* talking to a lot of people who believed that Pele, the volcano goddess, caused the eruption.

As their homes went up in flames they said things like "This is Pele's land, always has been." Ted kept asking why the government hadn't built retaining walls or dams to divert the lava—"We're dealing with a mass that is hard to comprehend," a scientist tried to explain. "It's so massive, so powerful, that you want to believe some kind of power . . . We're used to dealing with things in square feet, steel—this is so massive there's nothing you can do except step aside and let nature take its course."

Harry Kim, Hawaii's civil defense director, loomed up on the screen and Ted asked him if the town of Kalapana was "finished."

"Only the land and the buildings," said Kim. "The land has changed its form. The oceans will be the same, and that's part of Kalapana. The town, the buildings, are finished, but Kalapana will be forever."

By now Ted wore a look of bemused exasperation, which only grew as he listened to a native Hawaiian professor from the local university explain that Pele's body was the volcano itself. "It is her private parts, that she is giving birth from."

I have hiked around the volcano area—seen the lava flowing into the sea, where it hardens into acres of new land, seen the thousands of vents wafting steam up from the depths. It is dramatic and violent and beautiful—no native of the island could *not* have believed in a volcano goddess. But now? Now that we know how volcanoes work? Ted asked the white scientist from the federal government's nearby volcanological observatory to comment on this Pele stuff. "I think anyone who has worked around the lava flow has a feeling that there is a power out there that is greater than ourselves, and that is greater than something we can quantify with our numbers and the data we collect," she said. "There is nothing about Pele that is incompatible with science."

Science hasn't undermined the feeling that God is present in the natural world—if anything, it's sharpened it, shown the scientists ever more sharply the limits of human understanding, continually increased their respect for the harmony around us. The *Times* recently ran a long interview with Dr. Allan Sandage, the grand old man of cosmology who has spent his life in the hardheaded search for two numbers—Hubble's constant, which will reveal how fast the universe is expanding; and the rate at which it is decelerating, known as "omega," which will determine whether it eventually collapses back in on itself. He spends his time with big telescopes and bigger computers, and in crusty battles with his colleagues. "You weren't anybody in astronomy if Sandage hadn't stopped speaking to you at one time or another," a journalist said. And yet, like so many of the truly great scientists before him, he focused so sharply on the material world that the divine stood out in clear relief. He believed in the big bang, of course, not a literal Adam and Eve, but he also insisted that "science cannot answer the deepest questions. As soon as you ask why is there something instead of nothing, you have gone beyond science. I find it quite improbable that such order came out of chaos. There has to be some organizing principle. God to me is a mystery, but is the explanation for the miracle of existence, why there is something instead of nothing."

Still, there is a way that science *has* helped to amputate our understanding of the world as a sacred place. Not through explanation—that only illuminates the real wonder. But inadvertently, through the inventions its findings make possible. New technologies have removed from most of us in the Western world any need to spend time in contact with the physical, and hence erased much of the chance to experience the divine in its grandest manifestations. Consider the car. When a scientist studies combustion, he peers though his instruments at one of the million aspects of the one great mystery. But when someone takes his findings and uses them to build a Pontiac, he helps to insulate us from those mysteries, from the contact with earth and air and water that comes with walking, or the communion with other life that is part and parcel of the horse and buggy. Through her telescope or her microscope or her oscilloscope the researcher sees the inevitable numinousness of the planet—science expands her vision. Through our windshields we see road signs and taillights—technology has blinkered us. Convenience always carries costs—this one may be worth paying, but it is high.

Here on the mountain some hawks are circling, riding a thermal, looking for prey; the trees are bending in the wind, leaves dropping into the creek among the bugs. Everywhere I look I see: Down, on a patch a rock maybe a foot square, there's a big insect on improbable stiltish legs, and a patch of moss that is slowly building up a bank of soil behind it, and a carpet of dead needles beneath the wavy bottom bough of a Scotch pine. Up, at the horizon, there's an ocean of hills, round on top like this one—no homes, just hills, some with pines and some with maples. This expansive, wild world is not just the stuff of Druid ritual—it's part of most of the younger religions, too. The book of Job, for instance, the Bible's greatest poetry, tells the story of a man who suffers. He suffers not because he has done something wrong, or shown insufficient faith, or performed too few good works, but because he is a human being and we all suffer. His cry to God for an explanation, for a *reason*, is the eternal human cry. But when God answers, he says nothing about justice or fairness or singing "We Are the Circumcision." Instead, he just talks—boasts—about the beauty and the *rightness* of his natural world, and about its inscrutability. "Do you hunt game for the lioness and feed her ravenous cubs when they crouch in their den, impatient, or lie in ambush in the thicket? Who finds her prey at nightfall when her cubs are aching with hunger?" God invokes the hail and the snow and the wind, the rain and the light and the dark, the antelope giving birth, the wild ass scouring the hills "in search of anything green," the ostrich so stupid she'll break her own eggs yet "when she spreads her wings to run she laughs at the horse and rider." The world is suffused with meaningful, purposeful beauty, but its meaning and purpose are not human—"Why do you think I make it rain where there are no people?" asks God. Job is satisfied with this strange set of answers—it does not seem mysterious to him, or evasive, or insufficient. All these things are good, even when they are harsh, even when they make no human sense.

This information about the divine makes perfect sense on the mountain; it accords with what you feel, or at least what I feel and what many humans in many places have felt. That rightness, down to the sound of breath in your own lungs, can't come through the human mediation of a television set. It comes through the mountain, the field, the ocean, the sky, the tree, the animal, through gravity and heat and motion—it is information, pure and simple. It's potentially vital information—if we felt it down to the soles of our feet we might be more moved to protect the rightness, the integrity, of the planet. And because they're heirs to this feeling, the religious communities offer great promise for the environmental movement—those temples that haven't succumbed to Tiltonism are among the few institutions potentially capable of elevating and celebrating sacrifice, or embracing some goal besides the human material progress that is slowly choking the planet. But the crucial information, the feeling of rightness, grows ever fainter; and the more we wound the planet, the harder it will be to find, even for those who still seek after it.

4:13 P.M.

The jovial anchorman on the local news reaches into the pocket of his blazer and extracts a fortune cookie. He breaks it, retrieves the fortune. " 'There's going to be a cloud over your head.' Does that sound about right, Doug?' " Doug, the weatherman, is standing on the roof of the building against a gray sky, holding a folding chair at arm's length as if he were a lion tamer. "You're not going to like this forecast," he says. "I brought a chair out here with me, because it's going to rain tomorrow and Saturday and Sunday."

"So you don't want us to knock you off the roof?" says the anchorman.

"That's right," says Doug, who then interrupts his forecast to point at some people on the roof across the street. "That's the German military mission. Hiii, guys! Those are some German military officers." Returning to the weather, he details the weekend outlook—"no major improvements," "not at all encouraging," as if he were a doctor and the climate were in a coma. "To add insult to injury, we're looking at the possibility of much cooler weather. In one of the discussions on the computer today, a very nasty four-letter word was used to describe possible weather by the first part of next week in West Virginia."

"If we guessed that the first letter was 's' and last letter was 'w,' would we be close?" asks the anchorwoman.

"And in the middle was 'no'?" says the anchorman with the fortune cookie.

"I'll leave that for Bill to deal with in the next forecast," says the weatherman coyly. "Don't come up here and get me; I've got my chair."

Everyone knows, at some level, that the sharp line between "good weather" and "bad weather" is a fiction, that we need rain as surely as we need sun. Weathermen, despite their often aberrant personalities, usually have a sound meteorological education and know this better than most of us. And yet, almost without exception, they obey the convention that clear blue skies are good and precipitation is not. On the ABC affiliate the day begins with the *FUNCAST,* when the weatherman says it's going to rain and then uses hieroglyphs to describe what this will mean, apparently for viewers who have never experienced rain. Next to a drawing of a car there is one thumb up and one thumb down, which means the weather for driving will be only okay. Next to a picnic basket, a thumb down—don't eat outdoors in a storm. Topper Shott, the morning meteorologist on the local CBS station, rated each day as if he were a movie critic or a figure-skating judge. Friday, he said, would score a 5.5 on a scale of 10, up from a flat 5 the day before.

This convention interests me mainly because it is so similar to another commonplace of the news. "There's good news on the economic scene," an announcer said in the local newsbreak during the CBS morning news. "A report by the Greater Washington Research Center says the Washington area will soon resume the rapid economic and population growth it has experienced in recent years." On *Nation's Business Today*, which occupies ESPN until it's time for *Monster Trucks*, the announcer is just as cheerful: "yesterday's big jump in the leading indicators," plus an "encouraging" purchasing manager's report, helped send the Dow up, and the Fed has issued its Beige Book, which indicates that "the expanding economy is not placing upwards pressure on prices." All was not sunny, however; though this predated the 1990–91 recession by about three months, storm clouds were already on the horizon. "The International Monetary Fund is meeting this week," said an ABC newswoman. "It's worried about the world economy, estimating it will grow only 2.5 percent this year, the worst since 1982." From South Korea came footage of angry investors kicking down brokerage doors and beating up securities traders—used to double-digit growth, the country saw its gross national product expand "only 6.7 percent last year." An expanding economy, in other words, draws exactly the same smiles as a blue-sky forecast; a slowdown in global economic growth, to the point where it expands just 2.5 percent annually (doubing in size, that is, in about 28 years) is as ominous as the chance of a West Virginia snowstorm. And in this case it isn't half tongue-in-cheek. No one says, "Well, we do need the rain." (In fact, a new reason to dislike rain is that it disrupts the economy. Flooding in Texas, said one ABC newsman, was causing "Walmart to report lower sales.") If there is any one subject on which everyone seems to agree, any one point of doctrine to which every political sect subscribes, it's that "economic growth" is the highest goal, our ultimate goal as a country.

And not only as a country—as states, as communities, as corporations, as individuals. It's our great shared aim, and the examples from just this one day of television are nearly infinite. Virginia's Governor Wilder, for instance, held a press conference before he left on a trip to California, where he was going to woo the film industry ("Just knowing that Virginia exists is an important element") and try to convince the Japanese firm that had recently built a noodle factory in Sheffield County that it was time to expand it. He talked at enormous length about "the new mainstream," which meant balancing a number of tasks, such as "cleaning the air," with economic growth.

A clever AT&T ad began with some people carefully

building bicycles. They had a fine little company but it was not enough. "Our business had never been better," said one of them. "So one day we just looked at each other and knew—it was time to go public." They quickly utilized a lot of AT&T services, especially international video teleconferencing, which let them beg for money from a gracious German and a merry Japanese. The shining moment—replacing the pride of making bicycles—came at the end when they finally saw their new corporate symbol come zipping across the electronic ticker.

For individuals, financial expansion and growth go just as unchallenged. "Do you want to make more money?" repeatedly asked the spokeswoman for a trade school whose curriculum covers everything from gunsmithing to personal computing. "Sure—who doesn't?" she answers herself. "If you have a better mind and more knowledge, you can make more money," promises Kevin Trudeau, who is making more money by selling Mega Memory ("Memory techniques go back to the time of Julius Caesar") for only $59.95. This love of economic growth begins at an early age—the ads for Topps baseball cards opened with a towheaded boy saying, "The two 1990 baseball cards I bought for six cents are already worth three dollars." An older boy chimes in—"My Topps Mattingly rookie card? Already worth twenty-seven dollars!" The first child returns surrounded by friends. "But we collect Topps only for the fun of it, right, guys?" Everyone is smirking, rolling his eyes, laughing up his sleeve. "Topps," says the announcer. "Preferred by professional collectors—and professional kids." These ads work, by the way—a recent article in *Investment Vision* said that "the Beckett Baseball Card Monthly price guide has come to dominate the discourse of American boys in ways the editors of the Wall Street Journal can only dream of. . . . Launched only six years ago with a circulation of around ten thousand copies, the publication now entertains an audience of nearly a million loyal readers, more than half of whom are under sixteen." Sentiment is fine, but capital appreciation! "There's something magical about babies," warbled an incessant ad for Jessica, a porcelain baby doll from the Ashton-Drake Galleries. Her "playful pose will last forever," but perhaps you'd also be interested to know that "other dolls by the same artist have appreciated in value as much as a hundred and forty-six percent."

There is nothing odd about any of this, of course—it's how it's all supposed to work. People acquire more money, and buy more things with it, and the economy grows, creating more jobs and more prosperity, and so it has been since at least the Industrial Revolution. Growth in income, growth in consumption, growth in convenience and comfort—all seem absolutely obvious to us, as obvious that a beautiful day is a sunny day.

For some Americans, struggling to carve out a decent life, the logic really *is* logic. For many more of us, already comfortable by any global or historical standard, it is simply a given. "Do you want to make more money? Sure, who doesn't?" We understand this idea in our hearts—understand it so intuitively that no one needs to explain it for us (although, on one of the channels where you can take telecourses for credit, a USC professor does: "In a larger sense, what is the purpose of production? Well, we like to think that the purpose is to assist us in achieving higher and higher standards of living"). It's the idea we recommend, both directly and by example, to everyone else—*World Monitor* on the Discovery Channel carries a report from Cambodia, where economic activity is picking up, at least in Phnom Penh. But now the government has decided to "wean the economy" from its agricultural base with a "new industrial plan" featuring, among other things, Japanese lumber mills. "Mere self-sufficiency has not been enough to help peasants keep up with economic growth in the cities." This desire makes a good deal of emotional and perhaps even practical sense in Cambodia, where people have an annual average income of $103. The question is, does it make sense for us any longer—is it automatically cheerful news that the American economy is busily expanding? Or, like Californians in a drought, should we perhaps raise the tops on our convertibles and welcome a little rain?

Such questions remain heretical, but the heresy gains new adherents constantly, and not just among Thoreauvian cranks. Their numbers are not yet large enough that they make any dent in the momentum of society or raise a wrinkle on the smooth-browed anchorman. Still, our society's shiny faith in endless material progress has begun to tarnish. Many of the most subversive challenges have come from environmentalists, who question one of the givens of growth—that it will always be physically possible on a finite earth. At first, two decades ago, environmentalists predicted we would run out of certain raw materials. While over the long run this remains likely (it's awfully hard to believe that there's enough stuff for everyone on the planet to live the way Americans live), it seems unlikely that it will happen very fast. The newer and bigger fear is that the human pursuit of growth will go so well that its by-products will crowd us out. The greenhouse effect offers the best example of this line of reasoning: most growth now, and in the decades to come before renewable sources will make a large dent, will be powered by consumption of fossil fuel. (Here at home we can theoretically grow some without using more energy because we have so much waste to conserve, but that is not the case in, say, China, which is still near the bottom of its industrial slope—and rich with cheap coal.) Every time you burn coal, oil, or gas you release carbon dioxide into the atmosphere—five and a half pounds of carbon for every gallon of gas you use. There is no filter you can put on your car engine or your smokestack to reduce this flow of carbon dioxide, which acts as an insulating blanket around the planet; as it starts to heat the atmosphere we can expect disruptions of every physical system from ice caps to ocean marshes to cornfields. That is to say, a failure to change, in the very near future, from economies dependent on economic growth to sustainable economies, may turn the world we know into a forbidding, strained, and scary place. And it's not simply the greenhouse effect. If it did nothing else, a growing human population, using ever more resources and taking up ever more space, would inevitably crowd out much of the other life on earth. We could conceivably escape disaster, but we seem destined, absent real change, for ecological impoverishment.

A shift in a different direction would require a certain amount of sacrifice—a sacrifice at least of the idea that we should forever expect more and better. It would also demand a willingness to share what we have, both in wealth and technology, with people like Cambodians so their path to a decent life doesn't require cutting down all their forests and sending them to Japan. Sacrifices of this sort are not popular; therefore, the more "responsible" environmentalists always make it clear they're for more of *everything*—growth *and* protection. William Reilly, President Bush's director of the Environmental Protection Agency, spoke to a conference of foreign dignitaries on May 3, and his speech was carried on C-SPAN. He began by comparing Earth Day 1990, which had taken place only a month before, with Earth Day 1970. The 1970 event, he said, was "industrophobic," and had "antigovernment, antiauthority manifestations," whereas "what was most notable this time was the positive, enthusiastic, even exuberant mood of the crowds, the celebratory character of most of the speeches." He went on to laud the success of those twenty years (successes that the motley, bitter crowds of 1970 can apparently claim no credit for). The Potomac was clean again, a haven for windsurfers, and certain airborne pollutants had fallen sharply. Granted, there were still problems—something called "planetary stabilization," which seemed to be about the fact that the climate was changing and the ozone layer eroding. But he was confident that they could be dealt with the same way—"it was the engine of the economy, the growth in GNP, that created the wealth that paid for our cleanup," he said. We have to "craft environmental policies that do in fact reinforce economic development."

The result of this kind of thinking became clear when you listened to Linda Stuntz, the deputy under secretary of energy for policy, planning, and analysis, on another C-SPAN program that morning. She was hard at work on the "national energy strategy," which was going to "balance our need for energy at reasonable prices," "our goal to reduce dependence . . . on potentially unreliable energy supplies," "our determination to maintain an economy second to none," and "our commitment to a safer and healthier environment." That happy-sounding strategy, when it was formally delivered nine months later by the Bush administration in the winter of 1991, featured opening up the Arctic National Wildlife Refuge to oil drillers and treated conservation as if it were a crackpot scheme like perpetual motion; the president said he'd veto any legislation asking for even moderate improvements in automobile efficiency. Environmentalists expressed "shock" and "outrage," but the energy plan was the inevitable result of placing economic growth on an altar and making all else bow before it.

Until it becomes very, very hot indeed, though, I doubt if concern for Our Doomed Planet will force any real change in our economic habits. But there's another challenge to this idea of material progress, of endless economic growth, that occurred to me as I reclined in front of the TV watching the history of the last forty years. And that challenge is a simple one—things *aren't* progressing. I don't mean that we're not getting richer (though we're not—between 1969 and 1989, median family income in constant dollars rose only $562, from $28,344 to $28,906). I mean that even if, as the society urges, we all made twice as much money, our cash could buy us very little additional ease or even luxury. Daily life *has scarcely changed* between 1960, when I was born, and the present.

Which is not to say that progress never changed things. In a report about Vancouver turning a hundred, there was an interview with a woman, now in a nursing home, who had been born there shortly before the city was founded, when it was a circle of shacks. In her lifetime *everything* changed. People learned to talk across long distances on telephones, to travel easily and routinely. School became standard, even in remote areas. The occupations divided and specialized, replacing self-sufficient ways of life. Appliances transformed the home. Birth control allowed limits on reproduction. Easy refrigeration changed the way we thought about food. Most people's bathrooms moved indoors. People washed their bodies daily, not weekly. Medicine eliminated most childhood deaths, and made all lives healthier and more secure. Radio and then television spread a universal culture. Farming mechanized to the point where most people were freed from the soil. Some of these revolutions may have had dark sides—as I have tried to show, it is an uncertain liberation to be "freed from the soil," and universal culture may not satisfy in the ways local culture did, and routine transportation may have cheapened the geography of our lives. But the important point is that all these changes affected daily life enormously—and all of them took place before 1960.

Max Kampelman, formerly a senior arms negotiator, addressed a talk-show audience on the topic of progress, speaking in familiar terms. "I lived in a day when there were no vitamin tablets, no telephones, no man-made fibers," he said. "Things that are an integral part of our lives today. No airplanes. In no period in the world's development have so many changes taken place." And he's right—but he was born in 1920. The period of these changes was not his life, but the first half of his life. When I was born, we had telephones—we even had push-button telephones. We had airplanes—we even had jets. We had vitamin tablets—we even had doctors telling us that eating a healthy diet made more sense than gulping pills. We had computers, though they were huge and not so powerful. They have improved and shrunk enormously in the decades since, and yet they have made surprisingly little difference in daily life outside the office. If people use them at home, they are either toys or efficient typewriters; at work they have replaced some kinds of tedium and created others, but most of the major features of corporate life were firmly in place by 1960. Certainly every study shows that the amount of leisure time has decreased tremendously in the last thirty years, so computers aren't freeing us from labor. (Nor from paper and ink—pen sales grew 12 percent in 1990 to a record $3.25 billion.)

TV itself has gotten sharper and clearer since 1960. We have huge screens and tiny screens and a hundred channels of cable, and yet we watch about the same amount of TV, and many of the same programs. Jets are faster, but going from New York to Tokyo in half a day instead of a full day hardly counts as a dramatic change even in the lives of those who make the trip regularly—the dramatic change came when we could travel predictably to Tokyo without hitting, say, China, and, later, when we could do it as a matter of course in a day or two. Medicine is more powerful, and yet life expectancy hardly budges. We have microwaves, but we know they are just faster ovens—an increment of convenience (and perhaps a small sacrifice of taste and appearance) but certainly not a change in our lives. Molly Daly is a hostess on the QVC Channel, constantly encouraging people to upgrade their lives: "I look at phones nowadays, and I think of my grandmother's princess phone. Back then in the fifties even *a color* for a phone was rare. And we just thought that was the neatest thing since sliced bread." Now we have a phone in many colors, and surprising, appealing shapes. A phone that looks like a football helmet! A phone in the car! Do they change our lives?

We've gone through several musical changes—from the hi-fi to the stereo, with a brief excursion into eight-track (Country Music Television carried ads for the only item still being offered in eight-track, a collection of *50 Trucker Songs,* many of which recalled the even briefer infatuation with CB radios), and then onto compact discs. There's plenty of debate about whether a compact disc even sounds better, but it clearly still leaves you listening to high-quality mechanical reproductions of other people's music, as will digital audio tape and mini-CD and whatever else follows. I was reading an airline magazine recently and came across an interview with Dick Knowlton, president and CEO of Hormel meats. "We looked at the market and asked what could be competitive? What could be original? That's our main key in everything we do." Original, which at one point meant putting meat in a can so it could keep forever and calling it Spam (dubious, but original) now meant Spam Strips. It meant "microwaveable bacon packaged in individual servings of four with a self-opening feature that helps eliminate the grease encountered when cooking bacon." It means Frank 'n' Stuff!—"While developing Frank 'n' Stuff we designed, built and patented a system where we could put a perfect tunnel of chili or cheese in every wiener. So it made a point of difference with all the others."

Here's the proof. You can watch TV shows that are thirty years old without any real culture shock. Big changes have taken place—the semi-emancipation of minorities and women, the fall of the Communist empire, and so forth. But in material terms life on a 1960s sitcom closely mirrors life on a 1990s sitcom. If you walked into Samantha's kitchen in *Bewitched*, you would know how to make breakfast. In fact, you'd use many of the same products—it's almost eerie, for instance, that the same sugary breakfast cereals that rotted my teeth still rot the teeth of American youth. The bird is still cuckoo for Cocoa Puffs, the rabbit still finds to his immense sadness that Trix are for kids. (The one *new* breakfast development of my lifetime—Tang, the slurry orange juice of astronauts—seems to have all but disappeared.) If you walked into Tabitha's playroom,. you'd recognize most of the toys—Barbie, for sure. (The ideal of feminine beauty has not appreciably shifted—Barbie's measurements remain standard.) She would probably have a Nintendo, which is new. But a modern kid who turned on her TV (after searching fruitlessly for the remote control) would recognize the Mickey Mouse Club from its new incarnation, although the Mouseketeers now have good nineties names: Chase, Deedee, Lindsey, Marc, Jennifer, Josh, Brandy, Alana, Jason, Tiffany, Damon. Even the clothes in the closet would be more or less familiar—a 1990s Samantha might not dress quite so much like a Coffee-Tea-or-Me stewardess, and she might have tossed out the various miracle synthetics in favor of cotton, but that's it. Her social life might well have changed, too—she'd probably have a career and on her way to work she might have to step over homeless people. But the world of artifacts would be remarkably static.

If you did a similar experiment in, say, 1950, returning to the average American home of 1920, the changes would be staggering. It's that time of rapid progress we're really thinking about when we tell ourselves stories about the dynamic twentieth century. By contrast, the memories of people my age are spookily familiar. A hostess on one of the shopping channels was urging viewers to buy TV trays—"I have very vivid memories of when my grandmother got her first TV trays," she said, her eyes misting. Or as country music crooner Mac McAnally sang in a deeply nostalgic song about his Mississippi hometown, "TVs, they were black-and-white, back where I come from."

To continue believing that this is all so shiny and exciting, we have to pretend that we're people we're not. Kentucky Fried Chicken was running an ad in the spring of 1990 that showed a Russian woman in a babushka arriving in the United States for a visit. Her hosts immediately took her to a shoe store, where she marveled at the selection, and to a highway overpass, where she gawked at the stream of traffic, and to an appliance store, where she reverently opened and closed the door of a refrigerator. For dinner they all went to KFC, where she was predictably rapturous at her "first taste of America." Now, I've been to Russia, and this is precisely how a Russian would see our country—as a wonderland of well-made shoes and refrigerators you don't have to know a party hack to buy. A working consumer society is a joy (though fresh fruit would be more of a miracle to a Russian than fried meat). But this ad is not aimed at peasant women in babushkas—it's aimed at Americans, trying to make us feel as if it's somehow novel that we can buy refrigerators and fried chicken. That America is a new world of technological possibility! It's useful to remember that not everyone has what we have, and to resolve to share our bounty with Russians. But most Americans now alive have always had refrigerators, not to mention crowded freeways. For us this ad is emotional sleight of hand, not proof of progress.

Perhaps, though, this is just a plateau—perhaps we're about to take an escalator up some steep grade to some shiny new Nirvana, our lives as far superior to the lives of the Partridge Family as theirs were to the Neanderthals'. "Batman!" Commissioner Gordon is shouting in a rerun of the old TV series, which finds him in his first visit to the Bat Cave. "I feel like I've awakened in some future age! What wonderful machines! What fantastic ingenuity you and the Boy Wonder have employed in hooking it together." Or as Texas governor Ann Richards told a commencement crowd recently, "We are going to be creating a world that will make *Star Trek* look primitive." Perhaps—but probably not. Our trouble is that there's very little left in daily life to streamline. On *The Jetsons,* Elroy got his meals by pushing a button in the wall; a microwave oven, heating prepared entrées, is a reasonable facsimile. You can hook the microwave to a superconducting electric line; you can manufacture the entrée with genetic manipulation of cows and corn—it may be slightly more efficient, but in terms of day-to-day living it won't be much different.

The evening newscast on the CBS affiliate featured a new Mitsubishi picture phone—but this is a futuristic gadget we've been anticipating so long it already feels out of date, and now that it's here it's hard to see how it's really going to change your life. (It's even harder to see how it's going to improve it.) An ad, endlessly repeated, touts Glassmates, which makes it easier to remove fingerprints on glass and spots on mirrors. "Every day I clean them. *Spray* on the cleaner, *scrub* with one paper towel, *dry* with another. *Three messy steps,*" overcome with a single blow—these are the kind of dragons we have left to slay. CNN interviewed a scientist who once worked to crack the atom. He went on to develop the pat of butter, and now he's perfected a one-handed squeeze tube to replace the little envelopes you get ketchup in at Burger King. It offers "exquisite control"—he's writing "Hi CNN" in cream cheese. One of the shopping channels is selling lights that flick on and off when you clap—"This little idea is going to revolutionize everything we do." But this isn't even new! When I was a kid we had a device called the Whistle Switch that turned the TV on and off when you whistled. Or when you screamed—one night a friend of my father's got very drunk and stood in front of the set howling like a coyote. We finally disconnected it when it shut off the Rose Bowl during a thrilling touchdown run.

Most of these inventions are like that. *The New York Times* Living section had an article on new "smart houses" recently: "At home in the evening some people like to lower the window shades, dim the living room lights, and turn up the CD player. But why can't the house do those simple tasks itself?" Because who, save the severely disabled, can't lower a window shade or turn up the CD player? This is not like replacing walking with driving. It's not even like replacing the stick shift with an automatic transmission. It's like power-adjustable sideview mirrors.

Consider a *Newsweek* cover story on the future. (It appeared in 1980, and I saw it in Albert Borgmann's book, but it could have run last week—our material vision of the future keeps receding over the horizon.) "A revolution is underway," the magazine enthused. "But most of us perceive only dimly how pervasive and profound the changes of the next twenty years will be. We're at the dawn of the era of the smart machine—an 'information age' that will change forever the way an entire nation works, plays, travels, and even thinks." The writer then conducts a fanciful tour of this hearty new world: "Welcome! Always glad to show someone from the early '80s around the place. The biggest change, of course, is the smart machines—they're all around us. No need to be alarmed, they're very friendly. Can't imagine how you lived without them. The telephone, dear old thing, is giving a steady busy signal to a bill collector I'm avoiding. Unless he starts calling from a new number my phone doesn't know, he'll never get through. TURN OFF! Excuse me for shouting—almost forgot the bedroom TV was on. Let's see—anything else before we go? . . . Guess we're ready. Oh no, you won't need a key. We'll just program the lock to recognize your voice and let you in whenever you want." Even if we decide we want these things (I'm waiting eagerly for the first blackout, when six million suburbanites stand on the porch screaming at their doorknobs), and even if we can afford them (appropriate, surely, that our guide is ducking calls from a bill collector), it's clear it means no fundamental change and certainly no fundamental improvement. Survey data, by the way, show that a "higher proportion of Americans reported being very happy in 1957 than anytime since."

If we could accept this—if we could block out the assumption that economic expansion will fill our lives with sunshine—then perhaps we could begin to talk realistically about our predicament. Because it is a predicament—on the one hand continued economic growth threatens the environmental stability of the planet, but on the other hand the system we've rigged up requires constant acceleration or else it produces unemployment, misery, want. As

I write this, a year of recession—that is, a year of an already vast economy growing no larger—has created mild havoc. How do we step out of this trap? This is a debate we must have, I think—a debate about sustainability, about turning our efforts toward making sure that poor people have enough so that they don't need to destroy the environment, and that we don't have so much that we do it inadvertently. There have to be ways to accomplish this—a society that can develop the one-handed squeeze tube must have the brainpower to scale down while sustaining dignified and decent ways of life. It would not be easy—it would be as hard as anything we've ever done. But not impossible, except that the information comes at us so relentlessly: "There's good news on the economic scene—the Washington area will soon resume the rapid economic and population growth it has experienced in recent years."

The mountaintop offers eloquent testimony on all of this, for nothing there grows forever. There are no six-thousand-foot trees. Here's a red squirrel. When it was young it was tiny. It grew quickly. It stopped growing—if it continued, its weight would soon overwhelm its anatomy and it would collapse. (We know this about ourselves. If your three-year-old wasn't growing, you'd take him to the doctor. If your twenty-three-year-old grew a foot last year and seemed as if he were shooting for eighteen inches this year, you'd take him to the doctor, too.) The mountain offers a great deal of information about coming of age. It is settled, sustainable. On its own, without any outside inputs—without fertilizer or irrigation—it can run almost indefinitely, maintain itself at about the same size and density and composition. It has a correct size, a maturity. It doesn't seem to be lacking. You don't walk around saying, "We could squeeze a few more trees in there," or "Maybe the pond needs another boulder." It's fine—it's complete. But we haven't heeded this kind of silent witness, so now the physical world is sending us alerts. The increasing temperature, the thinning ozone—these are signals about the correct size of our society. Reminded hourly of our glittering destiny, though, we can hardly recognize them.

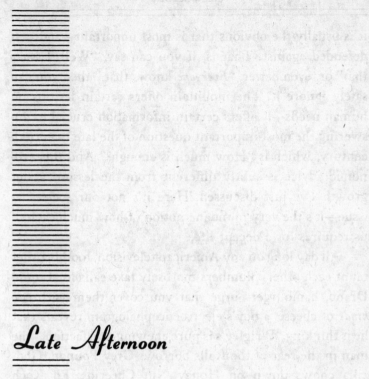

Late Afternoon

After climbing down from Blackberry, where I'd watched the vultures, I started back up the stream that led to the pond on Crow and to my tent. I was clambering contentedly along when all of a sudden I found myself out of strength and began looking for easy routes through the woods to avoid hauling myself up the rocks in the stream. I had eaten very little lunch, and I had hiked hard much of the day, and I seemed to be running out of fuel—a few handfuls of chocolate and nuts, and a few minutes' rest, revived my muscles and scared off the headache.

I want to indulge in one more burst of obviousness, for

it is usually the obvious that is most important—and best defended against. That is, if you can say, "Well, I *know* that" or, even better, "*Everyone* knows that," then you can safely ignore it. The mountain offers certain lessons on human needs—it offers certain information crucial to answering the most important question of the late twentieth century, which is "How much is enough?" And this economic advice is subtly different from the lessons about growth I've just discussed. Here it's not our society at issue—it's the very mundane notion of how much each of us requires for a decent life.

All day long on any American television, toothbrushes taunt each other, plumbers morosely take calls for Liquid Drano, hamburgers urge that you cover them with *two kinds* of cheese, a boy's electroencephalogram reveals that he is thinking "Wrigley's is pure chewing satisfaction," the man in the rear of the Rolls borrows Grey Poupon, Godzilla chows down on Honey Nut Cheerios, Ed Koch reduces, the disembodied Hamburger Helper sculls a gondola through the canals of Venice. Sophisticates all, we take it quite for granted that companies will tell us our emotional needs can be eased through purchases. ("Love you have to wait for. But Pantene you can just go get.") We'd be astounded if, as happened recently in Finland, a court ordered McDonald's to take an ad off the air. The commercial showed a boy who was sad about moving to a new home until he saw a Golden Arches across the street. This, the court ruled, "falsely leads people to believe that a Big Mac can replace friends and ease loneliness." But of course—that's the point of advertising. We're used to being told that a car equals frequent sexual relations, not a way to transport your body and your belongings around town. Perhaps you could even argue that this is good—that if your particular brand of beer makes you feel like a cowboy, or a tweedy professor in a bar, or a flat-bellied beach volleyball star, then it's an extra bonus.

A new trend is emerging, though, especially on the myriad unpolished cable channels that fill so much of the dial (not the dial, really—TVs have keypads now). On these channels—the shopping networks, the channels that devote half their day to the "infomercials"—you are more and more encouraged to buy simply because the very act of buying will make you feel good. It's quite early in the morning on *Home Shopping Spree,* and a toy panda named Bobo is wandering across the room. "He comes to you from China, where his real counterparts have lived for thousands of years," says the host, who then starts touting the Exertrack folding treadmill. "It has been *medically supported* that walking is one of the best exercises you can do." Lucia calls in from Long Island to buy one, and she chats with the announcer about his station. "It's very nice," she says. "You can get up at four-thirty in the morning and order something really nice."

Psychologists have been talking about "shopaholics" for some years now, and people have been wearing T-shirts that say "Shop till you drop," and debt counselors have been building big practices. But merchants have always thought it prudent at least to pretend their products satisfy a need—if not a physical need, then a psychological one. To some extent this pretense endures even on the shopping channels, though it grows balder. ("Are you bugged by something? Well, it just might be that your finger needs a diamond ring," said one shopping channel host. A few hours later, another saleslady described this picture of happiness: "You're wearing the ring on your finger, and driving in your car, kind of gazing at the ring, enjoying your drive, enjoying your ring. And then you get to the store, and maybe you're writing a check, and you just kind of put your hand down to write the check, and the girl behind the counter says, 'Whoa, beautiful jewelry.' And you say, 'Oh, yes, thank you. It's from QVC; it's for me!'") More and more, though, even the status and self-respect offered by the product takes a backseat to the pleasure of the moment of purchase. In a way, it has to. There's no tangible item for you to hold there on the shopping channels; gratification is delayed at least as long as it takes UPS to find you. But you can be part of the fun of *buying:* of calling in right before the *deadline,* of watching the host *lower* the price as the minutes tick on, of being included in the tote board that shows how many others have bought this item (in ten minutes more than *thirty-five hundred* people order the smokeless stovetop grill). Two of the QVC hostesses convene for a little chat.

Kathy: "Molly, I love to shop, in case you don't know that."

Molly: "Yeah, I think shopping is just an adaptation of the basic hunting instinct."

Kathy: "Yeah—kill, kill, kill!

Molly: "The bloodless hunt!"

The trailer for the smash hit *Pretty Woman* was shown over

and over on May 3—Richard Gere was telling the manager of a Rodeo Drive store, "We need some more people sucking up to us because we're going to be spending obscene amounts of money." Of course it's a joke, a pretty funny one. We all laugh, seeing ourselves. Only a society where the very idea of "need" had been banished could offer a market for, say, group captain and former Spitfire ace William Davis, who appears regularly to offer a coin commemorating the Battle of Britain. It's "valid legal tender" (in the Marshall Islands). Here's someone to sell a coat hanger that won't "rust and dirty your clothes!" (I have never seen a rusty coat hanger.) Already owning something is no reason not to buy it again—the Regina Housekeeper "makes an excellent second vacuum, maybe to put upstairs," and "you can't have enough white slacks—it's always a good idea to take a second pair with you when you're traveling," and "some Armani would be a nice gift, even if isn't his *main* fragrance." Pearle Vision *insists* that you need two pairs of glasses so that your frames can match your mood.

Buy so you'll have room to buy more—Rubbermaid produces the commercial that really sums up this phenomenon. "From the day I was born," a lady is saying, "I collected so much stuff." (The picture shows a sad family impossibly hemmed in by their possessions.) "So we stowed our stuff in stuff from Rubbermaid." (The house is now bare, save for big plastic boxes full of gear.) "Then we were so unstuffed— Hey! We need more stuff!" (Family charges happily out the door, waving hands in the air.) I remember reading with great interest as a boy about the decadent Romans, who would feast, excuse themselves for a short bout of feather-induced vomiting, and return to the table for another helping of hummingbird pie and whatever else it was that decadent Romans ate. Future schoolboys may look at tape of the shopping channels. They're a test of resistance, a siren song that eventually lures all who aren't lashed to their recliners. Watch them long enough and eventually you give in, go into a frenzy like the winners on *Supermarket Sweeps* who are stuffing lobsters up their shirts and steaks down their pants.

Even simpler than the shopping channels, even more primal, are the half-hour infomercials, which eat up vast chunks of the television day. State legislators and attorney generals and others of that ilk regularly introduce laws to drive these shows off the air, on the theory they are duping idiot consumers who believe they are "real" TV shows and not advertisements. I find this hard to believe, because the infomercials are so unabashedly enthusiastic about the process of selling. Their announcers, many of whom come from Europe (which seems still to command some vestigial deference), descend directly from the guys at the state fair demonstrating the new Miracle Juicer with eleventeen blades and three reverse gears. A few—especially the strange cassette courses to help you *Raise Drug Free Kids* or *Light His Fire* or study just *30 Days to Unlimited Success*—seem veiled and creepy. But most are likably obvious—exploded diagrams of desire. *Breakthroughs* opens with shots of cigarette boats jumping waves and girls in bikinis and Rolls-Royces, but then host Joe McKenzie gets serious. Today he's selling Dynafoam cleaning powder. Milt

Young, the president of Dynafoam, spends a few minutes demonstrating its utility—it can clean carpets and tile and mirrors! (Is there anything that can't clean mirrors?) But the real drama comes halfway through the show when it's time to announce the price.

"How much, Milt?" asks Joe.

"Three hundred and thirty-nine dollars and ninety-five cents," he says to gasps of disbelief. "No, no—you misunderstand," he says. "That's how much all the cleaning products it *replaces* would cost you to buy." He offers a price of $39.95, but the disgruntled audience still boos.

"Let me tell you how this works," says Joe. 'I've got millions of viewers out here in TV land who are waiting for me to bring them a breakthrough. I need you to sweeten this, to make a move."

"Well," says Milt, "in our warehouse we just happen to have a supply of those closet-expander coat hangers which can double, triple, even quadruple the size of your closet. I'm willing to throw one of them in."

"What about the other one you dropped on the floor."

"You're tough."

"I sure am. This is a big deal."

But the audience is still restive, even after he tosses in the second hanger *and* a Discover America Travel Package, which offers hotel discounts.

"I got to tell you," says Joe. "I'm relatively impressed. But we don't have a breakthrough. You have to dig down deep, to make it possible for millions and millions. Make the big move, make the grand gesture, do something outrageous. Make it happen."

"How many can I sell?" Milt asks.

"Give me the right deal and we'll sell millions."

The crowd, which knows its part because it never varies from show to show, is chanting "Breakthrough, Breakthrough, Breakthrough." Milt tosses in another bottle of Dynafoam and cuts the price ten dollars and it's done. The crowd roars. Joe smiles. Victory—it's not the Dynafoam we want, it's the deal.

None of this really bothers me—I have no wish to outlaw infomercials, nor to always buy only those items that I absolutely physically require. Even up on the mountain I was inordinately pleased with my fancy backpack, not because it carried my load better than other packs I've had but because it was sharp-looking and bespoke ruggedness and seriousness of purpose. There was no one else up there—it just spoke those things to me. Many of the old farmhouses around here, poor though they were, had marvelous grandfather clocks in the corner and those clocks meant not time but stability, family tradition, solidity. (Now QVC sells grandfather clocks for $89.50. "One of the nice things about it is this—most grandfather clocks, if you want to move them you need to get a couple of strong guys. This you can just lift.") Such possessions, even if we don't "need" them, can bring us real pleasure, and such pleasure is not something to be sneered at, especially if you have it under mild control. Some months later, at the start of the 1990 recession, I heard a woman on the radio say, with marvelous honesty, "Now, if there's something I don't need, I don't go right out and buy it."

So it is useful only in a limited sense to repeat Thoreau's famous calculation—to say that I lived on two dollars a day in food and fuel while I was on the mountain. Because as soon as I got off the mountain my expenses climbed again. It was instructive to remember for once that the reason I *needed* a roof was to keep the rain off my head, and the reason I *needed* that handful of chocolate was to fuel my body, and that the reason I *needed* a bed was that the ground was hard (though of course when you lack a Craftmatic adjustable bed, gravity still "exerts disturbing pressure on your internal organs"). The strict functionalism of the wilderness reminds you not to get carried away with psychological needs, to concentrate on what is real and necessary, especially in a world where excess consumption is dragging on the planet. But only saints and poor people can follow this rule with utter dedication—and often for poor people it is especially important to buy goods that carry status and solace even if they answer no bodily need. I have bought my share of stuff in the last few years that quickly wound up in the attic, and I'll likely buy more in the future.

This other kind of buying, though, the buying simply for the pleasure of the act itself—that the mountains can maybe help heal, in the way they used to help heal tuberculosis. What sets wilderness apart in the modern day is not that it's dangerous (it's almost certainly safer than any town or road) or that it's solitary (you can, so they say, be alone in in a crowded room) or full of exotic animals (there are more at the zoo). It's that five miles out in the woods you can't buy anything. There's no way to drive someplace and spend some money; you can't even phone a TV channel and place an order. I had seventy-five cents in my pocket, and all week it jangled. It may cost money to get there in the first place, but once you're there, commerce is utterly impossible. Having survived it, you emerge with a useful piece of information about yourself.

5:00 P.M.

Dance Party U.S.A. is at the beach today. Jetskis careen through the waves; onshore it's an hour of teenagers dancing nonstop to the hits of the moment. Almost all the boys are wearing jams and big breezy shirts; so are the few stout girls. The other girls are mostly in bikinis, or Lycra shorts, or something similar—the music never stops, and no one talks much. It's just an endless roving camera shot of young bodies—of breasts quivering, and butts, and thighs. Except for a few obvious ringers none of the dancers are professionals; most of them, in fact, aren't even very talented amateurs. As the hour wore on, a kind of trance seemed to settle over the action. In part, I think, this must have been due to the difficulty of strenuous dancing on loose sand. But the kids had, or so I imagined, a slightly baffled look, a what-am-I-doing-here? blankness in their eyes. Which is entirely appropriate, for in almost no other sphere have we managed to strip away meaning and information as thoroughly as in music and dance. Especially the music and dance that appears most often on television—the really popular stuff.

Music pounds from the television around the clock. Four networks—MTV, VH1, the Nashville network, and Country Music Television—devote themselves entirely to videos. And almost all this music and dance is popular—though the broadcast media began with classical music, it now has nearly vanished. I liked a lot of the hits everyone was playing—it's what I'm used to, the sort of music I grew up hearing. But it is popular, that is, "of the people," only in a peculiar and blanched fashion.

Music and dance, at their beginning and throughout most of their history, were drenched with content. On anthropological documentaries, they still are. Jamake Highwater, in a splendid show on the Discovery Channel, said that the Navajos danced to "make the sacred a visible part of life." An Indian, rigged with feathers, danced the eagle dance—it was, says Highwater, "performed for pleasure, but was also a tribute to the bird that is the holy of holies." Every traditional culture, writes Gary Snyder, "has its dance. The young people who come to the study of dance bring their perennial grace and power. They must learn to count the rhythm, memorize the plants, identify certain plants, observe the seasons, absorb the gestures of animals, and to move as timely as a falcon on a stoop. They thus are borne by their culture to become culture bearers." Dance and music ordered time; they passed down the stories that bound civilizations together. As Oscar Brown, Jr., said on a program called *Jumpstreet*, "For Africans, dance is for *functional* reasons—to honor birth, to mourn death, to celebrate harvest."

But by the end of the twentieth century, transposed to America, most of those functions have withered. The *forms* remain intact—Brown showed a sequence of grainy anthropological films of tribal dance intercut with *Soul Train* clips, and the resemblances were startling. But it wasn't about God or harvest or community anymore—it was about you shaking your proverbial booty. The George Mason University Channel covered a "stepping" contest between black fraternities—it's the intricate, semimartial dance celebrated by Spike Lee in his film *School Daze*, and, as the commentator explained, it's a "sophisticated societal experience of African dance." But its meaning on a suburban college campus is unclear, which is why the only thing to do with it is have a contest and some judges holding up scorecards. On an episode of the *Muppet Babies* cartoon show, a youthful Miss Piggy argued that dance should be "beautiful," by which she meant ballet. Skeeter, on the other hand, believed that dance should be "fun," by which he meant a sort of animated frug. The Muppet Babies view some film clips of Fred Astaire and then reach the predictable conclusion that dance should be *both* beautiful and fun. Which of course it should be—Fred Astaire belongs on any short list of American geniuses. But it can be, and almost always has been, something more than that.

The current emptiness is not television's fault, but television has made it visible—when you live in the age of videos there's not even a chance of ambiguity. The pictures are as much a part of the song as the tune—you're *told* what the music's about. Oprah's guests this afternoon were all songwriters, and at one point she turned to them and said, "How do you know what to write a song about?" Then she answered her own question: "There's only so many things you can sing about. If it weren't for love, what would we sing about?" Music has been slowly stripped of subject matter—most really popular songs are no longer about God or nature or work or anger or harvest or politics or death. There are plenty of exceptions, fine songwriters penning protest songs or brooding religious inquiries. But in popular culture the majority wins and if you spend twenty-four hours in front of MTV you will, I think, agree with Oprah that most of the lyrics, and even more of the visual images, concern themselves with romantic love. And even that veneer is falling away—they are about sex, really.

Dancing has always been sensual, of course, if for no other reason than that moving your body feels good. Fundamentalist preachers have long feared its potential for encouraging physical release and liberation. And there was a time when this liberation was real and necessary—the time when Elvis swiveled, maybe. But you can't be released when you are not bound, and by now sex has washed most other meaning out of the music. If you heard Billy Idol singing "Cradle of Love" on the radio, it might trigger many associations. But on video it is a leering "Cat in the Hat"—a girl in a miniskirt visits her neighbor, a lonely yuppie. She puts on the tape and turns into Thing 1 and Thing 2, breaking the furniture, ripping off most of her clothes, writhing on the bed to the beat of the music, kissing the confused neighbor, then flouncing off leaving him—and the viewer—hot and bothered. Now it's time for CLUB MTV, and Mr. Lee singing his hit "Pump That Body": "Houston, Pump that Body Minneapolis, Work that Body D.C., Pump that Body" Young MC is rapping "You're on a mission and you're wishing / someone could cure your lonely condition / looking for love in all the wrong places / no find girls, just ugly faces / From frustration first inclination / Is to become a monk and leave the situation / But every dark color has a lighter hope / So don't hang yourself with a celibate rope." The metal band Winger's new video features a girl on her hands and knees on a pool table—"I need your love, I need your skin, I need you baby to let me in." Lita Ford is straightforward—"I'm hungry for your sex"—and so is MTV: the "word of the week" on the channel is "callipygous," which means "having shapely buttocks," which every woman on MTV does. (They're encased, invariably, in tight black skirts.) I didn't, I suppose, spend as much time as I should have thinking how offensive this was. You can feel a little grubby watching it, but you watch—it knows what buttons to push. Were one video in twenty like "Cradle of Love," then maybe you could say, 'Well, that's part of life, sure.' But it's relentless—for hours on end that's pretty much all there is.

Big-time rock 'n' roll represents the zenith of this

trend—it's less apparent in the country music videos, which seem open to the idea that people can age gracefully or that love is as much emotion as instinct. And rap music, which appears here and there on MTV, has some of the feeling of older folk music—it clearly reflects a real, evolving community, and it carries a lot of information. But, at least in the videos airing this day, it was folk music refracted through television and consumer culture. Save for a few scattered howls at cops, the rappers stayed on ground familiar to most Americans. Their aspirations were almost entirely individual—to own brand-name consumer goods and to dominate women.

No, the most moving dance all day was on the Disney Channel. Two sandhill cranes were really pumping their bodies—up in the air and down, necks curving. It was foreplay, of course, as purely sexual as any Madonna video. But the narrator said they did this dance all year round, not just in the spring—that they did it "to reinforce lifelong pair bonds." It was about carrying on being cranes—if you were being anthropomorphic, you could say it was folk dance for cranes. It contained as much information, and therefore as much beauty, as cranes are capable of. It summed up the experience of being a crane—it was complete in a way that MTV isn't, because there's so much more to being human.

5:45 A.M.

I began the day determined not to write about the soap commercials. It is obviously well past the point of cliché that Madison Avenue uses great guile to sell copious amounts of cleaning fluids, powders, abrasives, bars, and pastes to Americans—anyone who has heard the term "soap opera" knows this to be case, so why mention it? But I've seen the same amazing ad at least a hundred times, and decided to break my vow. This commercial is on more frequently than any other by my rough count—it is for a new liquid called Jet-Dri that you add to your dishwasher during the rinse cycle. Why? Because "you can't always see it, but it's there. *Residue* from foods, detergent, minerals, clinging to everything your dishwasher washed." That is to say, your expensive appliance, which carefully sloshes soapy hot water and then clean hot water over your dishes, actually doesn't work. It leaves behind a "residue." You can't see this residue—it's *invisible.* But it's definitely threatening, because the ad shows a picture of a baby. This residue is the result of "detergent," of "minerals," of "food." Minerals? Aren't we supposed to have more of them in our diet? That's what One A Day insists. Food particles? How could invisible food particles hurt you? When they were visible you were eating them.

You don't have to be a bearded Viennese to wonder why a nation might be persuaded to invest in products that cleanse invisible and imaginary dirt, especially when the salesman is perverse enough to *admit* that the dirt is invisible. It's possible our nation's dark secrets have condemned us to this washing mania—that we are cleansing ourselves because we gave the Indians smallpox blankets or kept slaves or dropped the bomb. More likely, it's the invisible residue of our pseudoscientific fear of germs, combined with a greatly decreased contact with dirt. If you spend time on a mountaintop, you get dirty—you slip and soil sticks to your sweat, or you climb out of the tent at night to pee and the soles of your feet are in actual contact with the forest floor. Such exposure reminds you that dirt, after all, is not disease, or filth, or ordure, but simply the stuff of the planet. It does not harm you, and if you get more of it on you than you want you can almost always wash it off with water.

If you spend more time watching TV than wandering outdoors, you might end up writing letters to the newspaper like the one that appeared in the Q&A column of a recent issue of the Science section of *The New York Times:* "Does it hurt my dog to lap muddy water in the woods?" The *Times* consulted with an associate dean of a California veterinary school, who said it didn't. "Dogs lick mud off themselves all the time," he said, "just as children eat mud and dirt all the time without harm." I'm not *anti*-soap—when I climbed back down the mountain a hot shower felt great. But the volume of strong solvents that have been washed down sinks, and the number of empty plastic detergent jugs that have been tossed into dumps, and the amount of energy that it took to make it all, and the millions of vacant minutes spent staring at commercials—*there's* an invisible residue.

Late Afternoon

I can tell already there's not going to be much sunset tonight, just a long, slow deepening. First the light will lose its crispness, begin to soften. The sun, already dropping toward the horizon, will stand on the ridge above the pond, turning the trees to fire, and then duck beneath it—but even at that point there will be hours of twilight. Depending on how you reckon its start and close, dusk lasts for hours, just like "day" and "night." The sky turns from blue to another blue to another blue still—faster at the dome than around the edges, but always imperceptibly. Watching the whole process is hard if you have anything else you could be doing—reading a book or making a fire. It seems from minute to minute the same, as if you were staring at a painting. But a star is out now—for a long time only one, and then suddenly ten. Blue, still blue—but black now?

It has been a perfect summer day, warm and airy and spacious. The leaves are the deep matte green that imperceptibly replaces the illuminated green of spring. But on a few trees—sick ones mainly, though perhaps a few swamp maples too—a fringe of red has begun to show. And the night air, on the lightest breeze, seems to carry a small extra tang, a little more chill than the absence of the sun's heat would account for. And the blueberries have ripened; some have already withered. There is the sense of what is to come, that the slow rotation through the stars is carrying the mountain forward to the past, to yet another fall and winter and spring.

The question "What time is it?" draws a different answer on the mountain and in front of the TV. And the answers, far from being frivolous, have great environmental, social, personal meaning—the mountain and the television aren't so much in different time zones as in different dimensions. Human beings, of course, have perceived time in two main ways: linearly and cyclically. Either history advances forward through time or the world repeats endless cycles. These different conceptions are rich; they've spawned religions and philosophies for millennia. But, in truth, human beings were always exposed to both—any honest Buddhist has a personal sense of the course of his own current life, and even aggressively linear Christianity, with its sense of an approaching climax to history, is nonetheless soaked with the imagery of the seasons. In the last hundred years, though—and more and more all the time—the linear view is stomping out the other set of information, which is as old as man.

Take, just as one example, the length of the daylight hours. At the latitude where I live, nightfall varies by three or four hours over the course of a year. In December it's dark at four-thirty; at the end of June the light lingers late into the evening. This is one of the elemental pieces of information the world provides us—in other species it triggers dormancy and hibernation, the coloring of leaves and the gathering of food. Human beings always used to be sensitive to it—even after hours were invented, for millennia they were seasonal hours. That is, daylight was divided into twelve hours, as was dark—in the Northern Hemisphere, the period between, say, 1:00 and 2:00 P.M. was much longer during the summer than the winter. This piece of information proved too subtle for the mechanical clock, which in the thirteenth century began to smooth out time. But at least people still noticed the long, slow shift—felt it in their bones like the ancient pagans who built their elaborate monuments to mark the equinoxes and solstices. The spread of artificial light, and the ability to continue all activity around the clock, eroded this sense much more radically than the clock. Now we hardly even recognize the change—if it's pitch-dark or sunny out, the evening news still comes on at seven and "prime time" starts at eight.

Our *bodies* still notice the changes. CNN, *Good Morning America, CBS This Morning,* and the Discovery Channel all featured interviews with insomnia experts who prescribed fluorescent light therapy instead of Sominex. "Your body's internal functions respond to light, not to when you want to sleep," reported Dr. Charles Czeisler of the Circadian and Sleep Disorders Clinic. "People can work ten, twenty, thirty years on a night-shift schedule and their bodies never adjust." Despite the signals from our bodies, though, our heads, caught in the modern timelessness, win out—60 percent of Americans report "changing their sleeping habits so they can watch television." Prime time—the demarcation between the news/game show slot and the drama/comedy period—has almost certainly become the most significant line of the evening, replacing the evening star or the sun sinking beneath the horizon. TV doesn't even shut off for the night anymore: a few stations still carry "The Star-Spangled Banner" and a sermonette and then a test pattern, but most are eternal.

In much the same fashion, we ignore the progression of the seasons, the shift not only in hours of light but in climate. This once-dominant cycle has everywhere been flattened by technology. In Egypt, where the three seasons were Inundation, Sufficiency, and Deficiency, the dams on the Nile have made it always the same time. In North America, our aggressive heating and air-conditioning serve the same function—make the seasons, at most, something to observe through the windows. True, there were plenty of ads this day reminding you that the period for wearing skimpy clothing was approaching ("Summer's right around the corner—you should really start getting in shape"; "Lean Cuisine makes under three hundred calories taste like a million, and summer is the time to look like a million"), but these serve only to underscore how lightly we take the change from one season to the next. Even the school calendar has more effect on most Americans than the calendar of the the seasons—no longer farmers, we do not find it strange that we would make our new beginnings (introduce our new TV shows!) just before harvest.

But does this really matter? Blessed with light bulbs and dams, haven't we simply figured out a new, somewhat more efficient way to order our lives? We don't farm anymore, so why *should* we care much about the seasons or the length of the day? Because, I think, living in linear time means living with a different, and in many ways poorer, set of assumptions than living in cyclical time. On the mountain, feeling fall about to follow summer, I have a strong sense of what fall will be like—*fall,* not fall of 1991. The precise year, or the decade, matters little; it is a repeating pattern, and I know what it means for my life—that it's time to gather vegetables and can them, that it's time to put wood up for the winter. I know this fall won't be *precisely* the same as any other—a large part of rural conversation involves meticulous comparison of this year's snow or heat with the snow or heat of every other year. But I know they'll be *enough* alike, unless there is a storm so huge it changes the landscape. And even then how quickly the cycle reasserts itself.

A few economists, worried about the environment, have begun to talk about "sustainable societies," which instead of using more and more all the time use the same amount each year, an amount they can comfortably produce. I said earlier that I think this debate is the essential one of the years ahead—that we must wean ourselves from constant and accelerating growth. But this could occur only in cyclical time, when the years repeat themselves through the seasons—when each year spring offers a fresh start from zero, and the winter an obvious end. In linear time the late summer ("the third quarter") of 1991 seems remarkably different from the third quarter of 1990. It is a year later, and woe to you if you haven't kept up with the times. The third quarter of 1990 is useful not as a *model* but only as a baseline to measure your progress into the intervening twelve months. And the only acceptable result is to have more, because you don't know what's coming. It's not winter the way it's been winter all the times of your life—it's the first quarter of 1992, and that may bring something altogether unprecedented, requiring you to have more. Not enough to say that if on the first of March you have "half your wood and your hay, you'll make it safely through to May." Because May is the second quarter of 1992, a time that's never been before.

In such a world, constant acceleration becomes only normal, only reasonable. AT&T is running an ad where a boss demands that his subordinate call a client. He does, but because he is foolishly using the services of an AT&T competitor, it takes "as——long——as——this" to complete his call. It takes, to be exact, nine seconds, and he just misses the other party. These competing companies, the ads claim, are "up to forty percent slower"—that is, about three seconds. "This could add up to hundreds of wasted hours a year." (Actually it only adds up to an even two hundred hours if you make 240,000 calls annually, or 656 daily, or 82 an hour each day from nine to five.) Only a society obsessed with the linear passage of time would respond to an ad implying that going three seconds more slowly than technology permits might cost a guy his job. Viewed linearly, the rat race makes perfect sense—if there is a destination, you might as well get there first. But if, instead, you've internalized the seasons to the point where you realize you're on a wheel, you might slow down a little—might decide you're going nowhere impressively fast. If you're on a wheel, as mystics have long observed, speed is an illusion.

The most fascinating thing about dusk is the lack of demarcation. It's one long smooth transition. Really, the whole day is one long transition—there are a dozen parts of morning, and the moment in the midafternoon when the sun reaches its height, but almost before you can decide that that was the height the blaze has turned to glow. By contrast, life, especially TV life, seems constantly to insist on more lines, more borders. TV expects you to shift entirely each half hour—a whole new set of characters has appeared, and probably they're demanding laughter instead of fear or sadness. It should be a remarkably unsettling rhythm, except that now we're used to it, and the slow sprawl of the sunset, if we tried to watch it with real attention, would seem unsettling. We complain incessantly about the "fast pace of modern life," and say that we have "no time." But of course most of us have lots of time, or else every study wouldn't show that we watch three or four or five hours of television a day. It's that time the way it really works has come to bore us. Or at least make us nervous, the way that silence does, and so we need to shut it out. We fill time, instead of letting it fill us.

All of those changes make it hard for time to ever ripen. "In clock time," writes Kohak, "all times are uniform and arbitrary in their identity. Anything might be done at any of them with equal appropriateness or inappropriateness. There is no rightness, there are no seasons. Such patterns as life might have might well appear as no more than a convention, to be observed and violated at whim." That is to say, there is no rhythm—nothing like the image of summer following spring to help you orient yourself over the course of a lifetime. Which in turn makes it very strange to grow old and die. Almost no one talks about death on television, which is odd considering the number of corpses. (A rare exception was on one of the local public access channels where two agents demonstrated their sales pitches for viewers of *Insurance Corner.* "You've got to hit the hot button with the client, make them realize they *are* going to die," said one of the men. "That's right" said the other cheerfully. "The odds are one to one.")

People talk more about retirement on TV, but it clearly doesn't reflect a necessary season in people's lives, only a law—a transition as quick and brutal as *48 Hours* to *Falconcrest.* Its main consequence is not philosophical but financial—the time when you go from earning money to living off accumulation. So on television, "coming to terms" with aging inevitably means salting away cash, not wondering about death. The line between activity and retirement is as devoid of information as the line between

Twin Peaks and *Prime Time Live*—there's no reason anyone even attempts to give you as to why at sixty-five you should change your life. (One of the most interesting facts of the day came from a senior citizens' lobbyist who claimed that Bismarck set the retirement age at sixty-five after his actuaries told him almost all his bureaucrats would be dead by then, reducing the need for pensions. Sixty-five in Bismarck's time, he said, corresponds to one hundred and seventeen today.) The average American will spend two decades in "retirement," and since he is still operating on linear time, what is he to do? Act young, maybe—perhaps move into a "multiservice building" like the one prepared by Fairfax County where college kids are hired to teach you to dance to "Blame It on the Bossa Nova," or maybe buy cosmetics from Vikki LaMotta, the first over-fifty *Playboy* model, who has her own infomercial. But there is no cadence to make the approach of death less fearful. Maybe you'll just keep going, and Willard Scott will be saying, "Hi to Besse Hamilton, of Shreveport, who's two hundred sixty-two today—wotta pretty lady!" That must be our hope, since we fail to prepare for death—indeed fight against it with a strength that almost any other culture in almost any other time would have considered bizarre.

On the mountain, of course, death surrounds you always. Dead trees, the insects and the birds excavating their guts; dead leaves under your feet beginning to disintegrate with a year of rain and snow; dead bones in the woods where the coyotes hauled down a deer; dead shrubs where the beavers revised the level of the pond and flooded them out; the soil under your feet an enormous crypt holding the death of all the years since the Ice Age ended. And there is dying, too. Quick dying—the suddenly strangled cry of a rabbit in the night when something takes him down. And slow, patient dying: the maple sends out so few leaves this year that there is more sun than shade beneath it, and moss spreads up its slowly rotting trunk. And youth, of course shouldering up right next to age, vigor edging out gnarl—youth rooted in the death it will someday contribute to. You need not be an Eastern mystic anticipating physical rebirth to appreciate these cycles. This is the weary, austerely sublime wisdom of Ecclesiastes, too: "To everything there is a season, and a time for every purpose under heaven. A time to be born and a time to die." And that time to be born and to die is explicitly like the time to sow and to reap, to scatter and to gather. But we don't know those times anymore—it's harder and harder for us to imagine, as many people used to be able to divine, when our time has come.

What's worse, our culture won't lend us any dignity in those moments. For television, the culture's great instrument, speaks to eighty-year-olds and eighteen-year-olds with the same voice. I think of my grandmother, spending her last years remote control in hand. She could watch what she felt like, of course, but almost all the choices had been created for those with desirable demographics. Television never grows old, never ceases that small talk that may be innocuous when you're thirty but should be monstrous by the end of your life. Right to the last day of my grandmother's life it continued to offer her the sight of Donahue discussing sex changes and Cosby making faces and Vanna spinning letters.

8:00 P.M.

While I was resting by the pond, Saddam Hussein invaded Kuwait. I didn't know it at the time, of course—didn't know it until a few days later when I hiked out of the woods and my wife told me. My first impulse was to turn on the radio, and I kept in on for what seemed like most of the next six months. Though I started three days late, I soon spoke as confidently as everyone else of "elite republican guards" and Security Council resolutions and the history of the Baath party and playing the Israeli card and dug-in positions and smart bombs and Patriot missile launchers and chemical weapons capability and all the rest.

Here was the information age in its finest hour—all the world tuned into CNN, raw data not filtered through commercials or sitcoms streaming in real time around the globe.

A few months earlier, on May 3, very little of lasting significance happened—a slow news day. Not that that reduced the volume of coverage, however. TV's critics constantly complain about the lack of news and public affairs on TV, comparing it to a diet of junk food. In truth, there's a torrent of news—a steady force-feeding of slightly sugar-coated shredded wheat. The local CBS affiliate, WUSA, for instance, begins its day at six with an hour of local news, followed by two hours of *CBS This Morning.* From noon to twelve-thirty there's more local news, and it resumes again at 4:00 P.M., running for three solid hours until the Dan Rather broadcast at seven. The local news returns for half an hour at eleven, and from two to four in the morning the station airs *Nightwatch.* When it finishes, they air it again from four to six, when the local news resumes—that comes to eleven and a half hours daily. This was a Thursday, however, so add an hour for *48 Hours,* which focused on the victims of violent crime. And CBS, like the other networks, dutifully replaced most of Sally Jessy Raphael with live coverage of an excruciatingly dull presidential press conference, in which Mr. Bush made the unsurprising announcement that he wasn't going to upgrade a kind of missile called the Lance that was sitting in West Germany aimed at what very soon was not going to be East Germany anymore. In other words, WUSA offered more than thirteen hours of news.

Besides the networks, CNN and CNN *Headline News* provided twenty-four hours a day of coverage (in July of 1990—that is, before the Gulf War—52 percent of Americans already said they watched CNN regularly or occasionally), and a pair of videotext channels ran every Associated Press business and news story. A proliferation of pseudonews shows with vaguely suggestive titles—*Inside Edition, Hard Copy, A Current Affair,* and the like—competed all afternoon and evening to see who could find the most outrageous scam or lurid murder trial. (*A Current Affair* won hands down with its story about "a modern-day Jack the Ripper" who wrote poems about his "sanded, burning eyeballs" and sent them to his girlfriend, who, incidentally, was living with his wife.) Many of the various cable channels also ran "news updates" during the day. For instance, on *Lifetime,* which targets women, an anchorperson would come on for twenty seconds to tell about a new Danish drug that fights osteoporosis, while the USA network news update at 11:00 A.M. offered one story: "After six years, Burger King is dropping Pepsi and returning to Coke." Each of the colleges in the area also aired a newscast where students showed how well they had mastered the conventions of the profession. (Snappy transitions, for example: "In sports, Mother Nature beats the Dukes on the diamond. More coming up when we return.") This eerie slickness even enveloped the student-produced news from Fairhill Elementary School. "Yo, couch potatoes!" said a fifth grader. "It's time for the Couch Potato Movie Review—*Gods Must be Crazy II.*" (The Fairhill news team offered breaking stories, too. "Today for lunch you'll be having chicken nuggets with hot, flaky biscuits and choice of two: oven fries, fresh orange wedges, apple juice, chef's salad.")

And what exactly does all this information leave you with? Not, at least in my case, the feeling that I understood how the world had changed that day, much less how the world worked. The critics of television news, who are legion, usually fix on some particular problem. Maybe that big business owns the networks, so of course they don't want to rock the boat. Or that image has overwhelmed substance—if you ever doubted this, read Kiku Adatto's study, published in *The New Republic,* which compared coverage of the 1968 and 1988 presidential campaigns. In 1968 the average sound bite stretched 42.5 seconds; in 1988 it lasted 9.8 seconds.

Perhaps the greatest distortion of TV news, though, comes from the very fact of its seeming comprehensiveness. Each day it fills its allotted hours no matter what, and each day it fills them with crackling urgency. A newspaper comes out every day too, but a newspaper has a variety of ways of letting you know whether an event is important or not. The single most useful thing about *The New York Times* is that the width and type size of the lead headline each morning lets you know how it compares, in the view of the editors of the paper, to all the other lead stories since the *Times* began. It has a way to say to its readers "nothing earthshaking happened today; it's okay to read the reviews or the sports." TV has almost no flexibility of this sort. David Brinkley, on the night of the first satellite newscast, anchored the news from Paris. "Via Telstar," he announced, "there is no important news." I don't believe that this has happened since.

Something always happens, of course—this day it was President Bush's unsurprising announcement about missiles. Also, Lithuanian prime minister Prunskiene made a very inconclusive visit to the White House, where she and the president spoke a lot of diplomatic language, and former hostage Frank Reed waved at newsmen from the balcony of a military hospital in Wiesbaden, and a fire spread in the Everglades, and flooding in Texas swept away several cars, and the Dow closed up 6.53 at 2696.17, and contractors who outfitted Trump's Taj Mahal casino said he owed them $35 million, and an Amtrak train went off the tracks but not too disastrously. All in all, considering the twentieth century, a pretty calm day. No new wars, no massacres, no natural disasters causing deaths in the double digits, no startling turns of course. And yet from the severe look on Dan Rather's face you'd have thought he was FDR and it had been a day of infamy. The Bush administration, by its decision not to upgrade its missiles, was "bowing" to the new European order at a time when Gorbachev was trying to "strangle" Lithuania, and so on. By the end of the newscast, of course, he'd shed his wartime-leader face for his "Get a load of this" grin, as he does each night when it's time for the closing teaser story—this evening it concerned protests by Wellesley students over the choice of Barbara Bush as commencement speaker. It's not that the newscast was vapid—like each of the network newscasts it carried several decent feature stories. But there was no way to put them in perspective, and perspective is our chief need.

TV congratulates itself endlessly on its commitment to urgency. The promos and opening titles for nearly every local newscast showed their square-jawed personnel out battling the clock to bring back film, which was edited by rushing technicians while the heroic correspondents batted out copy on flashing screen—finally the anchor settled into the anchor throne, took a second to gather her breath, and then launched into her report. Such grace under pressure! Such valiance in pursuit of truth! It's the newsman as swashbuckling matinee idol, Luke Skywalker with a minicam. As it happened, *Broadcast News,* the 1987 film about a network news department, aired on Cinemax in the morning. Near the beginning of the film, Holly Hunter proves to the audience that she is a gritty, supremely competent producer by finishing the editing of a report on a soldier's return from the war with just seconds to spare—she has to race with breathless control not because it's breaking news or she's found a new detail, but because she wants to insert into the report a shot of a Norman Rockwell painting of a soldier coming home. It's not the substance that counts (the Rockwell is trite at best) but, as critic Todd Gitlin points out, the "style of substance," the feeling that this fluff has been pasted together with heart-stopping professionalism. (This scene is even paid careful homage in a commercial for Degree, a "body-heat-activated antiperspirant" that dries the secretions of harried TV producers.) The act of assembling the news is supposed to add a vital tang of drama to its delivery—it's as if you went to Dunkin' Donuts and the guy behind the counter thought you'd enjoy your breakfast more if he showed you a video of himself arriving in the predawn darkness to personally inject the jelly filling.

Some subjects suit themselves to this kind of jangle—all day TV provided excellent coverage of the flooding in Texas, gathering all the expected footage: policemen going down streets in rowboats, using bullhorns to persuade reluctant residents to evacuate their homes; families trucking their furniture away as the water rose; volunteers carrying old folks out of nursing homes; tired people huddled in school gymnasiums sipping Red Cross coffee and making plans to go home. TV excels at covering disasters, of course, both natural and human. Given a volcano, a massacre in an interesting country like China, or a police beating captured on videotape, TV will bring it home. The lava oozes toward the recliner; the nightstick thuds against the ottoman; the TV provides a great common reference.

But the worst disasters move much more slowly, and thereby sneak past the cameras. Consider two of the grinding glaciers that are slowly, patiently, methodically changing the topography of the world around us—the decay of the global environment and the wicked, miserable poverty that traps so much of the country and the planet. Everyone, including the people who produce news programs, recognizes the seriousness of these problems, and yet television fails to get them across—not to solve them, merely to make them understood.

This is in part because they happen on time scales

that defy television's relentless dailiness. Covering global warming, for instance, obviously matters more than covering a flood in Texas—its effects are a million times greater, and since we can take steps to prevent it there's reason to cover it. It's a little more complicated than the water rising till it goes over the top of the dam, but not a *lot* more complicated—any sixth grader can figure it out. The trouble is, the greenhouse effect doesn't change from day to day. The only points of entry for the story are heat waves and new scientific studies, and so this behemoth of stories pops up from time to time and lets out a growl. But we need to hear it roar. TV's vaunted immediacy is here a curse, and even newspapers can't help much—you need a book, or at least a documentary, to see time unfold over decades. Something that happens constantly and all around lulls the camera. You can't dash off in a helicopter to track down global warming—you need to sit calmly in a chair and think.

The story of poverty and its attendant sadnesses presents a slightly different problem. Here there is no shortage of hooks for stories. Every unemployment report or new set of data about infant mortality rates in the inner cities or fresh footage of famine in Africa offers another chance for a feature on young men who've never held a job or young mothers who've never been to a doctor or babies with swollen bellies. And TV tries to provide these stories—the criticism that it's interested only in "feel good" stories is simply wrong. But the medium is so big that each of these stories has to be about a class of people—young mothers and their problems, the woes of the chronically unemployed, the starving in Africa—instead of particular people. As a result, they dramatically understate the idiosyncratic and inherent messiness of human lives, especially lives lived under grinding stress.

On *Nine Broadcast Plaza,* for instance, an interview show on one of the superstations, the reporter was questioning three elderly people—Mr. R., Mrs. S., and Mrs. G.—who had been abused by their children. Each was wearing enormous black sunglasses, apparently in the belief that this would disguise them, and they were accompanied by their social workers. The host was in high dudgeon before the interviews even began, telling horror stories about "an explosion of violent abuse" that had left one unidentified woman so badly beaten they found her "with ants crawling through her wounds."

Unfortunately for the host, it turned out Mr. R. had not been hit by his son. "He never hurt me, he never hit me. Just talking. He'd say, 'I don't like you too much. . . . If you die I won't be at your funeral.' "

"Are you afraid of your son?" the host asked hopefully.

"Oh, no way, no way am I afraid."

Turning quickly to Mrs. C., the host asked, "Who's doing the abusing in your case?" Well, it turned out that no one was actually abusing her—her son was taking drugs and that was placing stress on her. "Have you had *physical symptoms* from this stress?" he demanded.

"They thought I had a heart attack, but I didn't," she said.

As for Mrs. S., her daughter was "a devil." By doing

"common labor" Mrs. S. had saved half a million dollars, she said. She bought a car for her son, one for herself, and two for her daughter, but her daughter still hated her and talked about having her committed.

By this time the host had turned in desperation to the social workers. "These are all stories of emotional abuse. That's just one type. *Physical abuse* can be even more devastating. What are some examples of that?"

Well, said one of them, "most are acts of omission and neglect."

The host listened for a while, and asked a few more questions, and before long he returned to his sunglassed elders. "Although your son never said 'I'm going to hit you,' you were led to believe he might hurt you. Where did you feel you could turn?" he asked Mr. R.

"Well, I don't believe he'd try to hurt me,' said Mr. R. "But you never can tell."

These people were quite clearly victims of tragedies. But they weren't the right tragedies, the ones scheduled for today. And they weren't the sort of tragedies that ever show up on TV, except maybe in the soap operas, because they're too particular. You need a novel to explain why Mr. R.'s son doesn't want to come to his funeral, and TV has no patience for novels—not even the small novels a good newspaper columnist provides. And without this novelistic sense of life's sloppiness, an awful lot of the solutions that we try to design will fail.

MacNeil and Lehrer devoted half of their evening newscast to "Growing Up in America," convening a panel of five adult experts. They were good people—one of them, Marion Wright Edelman of the Children's Defense Fund, is probably a saint. But almost all they wanted to talk about was whether or not the federal government was spending enough money on programs for children. Some thought yes, some thought no. Those who said we should spend more carried the day—a rich country that can't even inoculate its children convicts itself of serious crimes. But the subject of "Growing Up in America" is infinitely more complex than that. Growing up in America involves a dozen troubles—parents too busy and grandparents living in Arizona, the passage through adolescence in an atmosphere of commercialized and omnipresent sexuality, the pressure of keeping up appearances in a society obsessed with consumption, and so on.

You *can* get some sense from television of just how messy and complicated life can be, but only by doing whatever the electronic equivalent is of reading between the lines—looking in the corners, maybe. For instance, a lot of the late-night ads were clearly aimed at Washington's poor, not Fairfax's rich. Here's a company that lets you "rent to own" over a period of months. A Samsung TV-VCR is only $18.95 a week—by the time you own it you'll have paid $1,478.10 plus tax. They'll also rent you "gold jewelry" for $13.99 a week. "You need the respect a credit card can give you," advises the next ad—there's an almost palpable sense of endless financial strain, of constantly being short, of the understandable, warping desire for all that you see advertised each day. A young black man is advertising last-resort auto insurance—he's had seven accidents, he says with a rueful grin, and he hit a police car. "But my lady won't walk anywhere." Or turn on *Jeopardy*, and listen to contestants tell Alex Trebek what they do for a living—along with jury selection, this is one of the few moments when the lives of ordinary people are treated as if they are of interest. On tonight's program, Doug says his job "is to chase after ex-husbands who don't pay child support and alimony," and John helps companies look after "de-staffing," two professions that give you a sense of what's going on in parts of our society. Or watch the sign-off sermon on Channel 32, delivered by an aging black pastor. It's on the topic "Praising God Anyhow."

The grittiest show on all television appears on one of the religious channels—it's a call-in program called *Cope*, hosted by a kind woman named Dr. Karen J. Hayter. Tonight she's taking calls about depression. A woman phones in—she has a gun, she says, and she's probably going to kill herself. A week before, her alcoholic husband of twenty-four years had run her out of their house. She would have to leave her sister's house in a week. She had no money and no education. "My husband had many affairs, with his cousins and all," and had walked out of a treatment program—"He said he liked his marijuana and alcohol." She had wanted to make sure her children got their education, and her son had just graduated from high school, so now "death looked like the easy way out." So what do you say to this woman? Or to the woman whose father had committed suicide when she was five and then she'd been molested by his best friend, who was now her stepfather? Or to any of the others who called in, sobbing, from whatever trap the world had laid for them? Maybe the best you can do is tell them, as Dr. Hayter did, that God loved them, and that they should enroll in one of the many AA-type groups that have sprung up to create something resembling communities in the midst of our society. TV can handle each of these problems serially—that is, it can make a movie or a documentary or an after-school special about alcoholism or wife-beating or suicide or homelessness. But it can't handle the jumbled stew of troubles that makes up any impoverished life; because to do that would be to narrow the focus to a single ordinary experience, and the whole point of "broad"casting is just the opposite. Life can just be messy—here's a man phoning in to a tax expert on one of the cable channels to explain that he's divorced but now he's cohabiting with his ex. If he marries her again, would this year's alimony be deductible? (Yes, but she'd have to pay taxes on it.)

The relentless flood of information we receive, then, does not necessarily equal an understanding of our situation. The principal boast of electronic communication is speed, and speed doesn't help much in grasping these situations—it doesn't matter if you learn about the greenhouse effect this week or next week or next month. What matters is that when you do hear about it you understand it so deeply and thoroughly that you begin to question the way you live. It doesn't matter if you hear constantly, night after night, about poor children or abused elders. It matters that you hear about them in some way both deep enough and complicated enough that you'll go out and do something useful. Sometimes speed does count, of course—if you learn about starvation in Africa soon enough, you can stage a massive rock concert in time to spend the profits on milk powder. But even here the immediacy of television takes its toll. The famine in Africa in 1985, all the experts said, was as much a structural famine as a matter of crop failures; once the food aid arrived, the political infighting, development patterns, and environmental mismanagement of the region needed serious and prolonged attention. But when the starvation subsided, the cameras left, and with them the pressures from outside to do something. When starvation resumed in 1991, most of the cameras were elsewhere—in Kurdistan, or in Bangladesh. It's important that we see the effects of a cyclone in Bangladesh, but the real story is that a cyclone of poverty and overpopulation batters Bangladesh each and every day, and until it is somehow solved people will continue to build villages on floodplains.

Here's one way of asking the question—if instead of watching the news each night on television, or devouring the newspaper each morning, say you heard only one newscast a week, or read every third or fourth issue of *Newsweek.* If you reflected carefully on what you did read, I think in some ways you'd understand more about the planet. You'd still be more familiar with what was going on than almost any human being in history—you'd know about the gap between rich and poor, about ecological threats, about styles and trends, about political shifts and disasters. You'd know from repetition what really counted. And anything you didn't find out about—anything that flared up for just a day or two and then died out—couldn't matter much. I'm not seriously suggesting that anyone do this, of course—it takes a monumental act of will for most of us to remain in the dark even for a day or two. My wife and I live deep enough in the country that our paper comes a day late in the mail, which means we can skip whole stories, confident that whatever battle they describe has been superseded. But most evenings we tune in *All Things Considered* on the radio, and just its familiar theme music helps order the day.

Many of us tell ourselves that we need such constant updating so that we'll be able to cope with the "rapidly changing future." But it's not as if, by watching every moment of television, or reading every newspaper, you can really glimpse what the future holds. This May day came only three months before Saddam's invasion of Kuwait, the biggest news event in years, and no one even mentioned Iraq. Well, almost no one. A thin old man in a vested suit named Dr. Charles Taylor did appear on a program called *Bible Prophecy Today*, and he said that Iraq was trying to get a "nuclear trigger," and that it had a chemical capability, and that it would soon attack Israel—"in the fall is the most likely time." Dr. Taylor wasn't entirely right—he had Egypt on the wrong side, and he didn't know about Kuwait, and he said George Washington had had visions of nuclear attacks on America. But watching the tape of his confident analysis—"President Hussein has long harbored ambitions to dominate the region"—during the following winter as Scuds were slamming into Tel Aviv certainly added some zip to his tag line: "I'll see you next week—or

I'll see you in glory!" I don't mean that Dan Rather *should* have known that Saddam Hussein was going to invade Kuwait—*The New York Times* didn't know, and the State Department hadn't a clue, nor did the CIA. And Dr. Charles Taylor clearly had well-placed sources. I mean only that watching the news on the theory that you'll find out what's going to happen is like buying a truckload of Coke because one of the cans might be the million-dollar prize winner. It's remotely possible, but you'd be so sugar-bloated and caffeine-jangled by the time you got to it you'd likely not even notice. By the way, the only mention all day of the Stealth aircraft we'd soon come to know so well was in an ad for Thunderjets fruit snacks, which also come in the shape of F16s, F14 Tomcats, and MiG 27s.

It's undeniable that if you spent a lot of time on a mountain, or anywhere else distant from a tube, you might miss something. The even tone of the Emergency Broadcast System, which all children of the TV age intuitively know will be the last sound they hear before they die—you might miss that. But on a mountain, or anyplace well away from the noise of the world, there is room for reflection on what you *do* know. Who better understood the war in the Persian Gulf—the person who watched every nerve-jangling second of CNN's wraparound wall-to-wall coverage or some mythical person who heard only the most important points of the debate and had time to ponder? Some Denver researchers attempted to answer part of this question, and their findings, reported by Alexander Cockburn in the *San Francisco Examiner*, are suggestive. Knowledge of the facts of the conflict varied inversely with the amount of time spent watching the coverage—that is, only 16 percent of light viewers mistakenly believed Kuwait was a democracy, a fraction that increased to 32 percent among heavy viewers.

Even on a mountain you can't escape the news. Escaping the news is an ignoble goal—in a nuclear, damaged, suffering world what happens elsewhere is all of our business and all of our shame. Access to news of distant events is one of modernity's true miracles—in the last few years it has shaken tyrants and brought them down. But the people of Eastern Europe or China didn't rise up out of an intricate and detailed knowledge of daily events in our system—they knew that people elsewhere lived more freely, and much more easily, and those broad understandings helped encourage them in their revolt. And it's not as if *we* need to know every jot and tittle in order to act—cranky old Thoreau is a useful witness in this matter. He scorned those who kept fanatically up-to-date ("Hardly a man takes his half hour's nap after dinner but when he wakes he holds up his head and asks 'What's the news?' "). He ridiculed attempts to speed communication between continents ("Perchance the first news that will leak through into the broad, flapping American ear will be that the Princess Adelaide has the whooping cough"). And yet he knew enough about the world to act. He knew that the Mexican war was wrong, and on reflection knew it was wrong enough to require that he go to jail. His protest was not based on extensive reporting from Mexico—"Civil Disobedience" includes no list of atrocities from the front. His protest was based on small amounts of information fed, in long hours of wilderness reflection, through the mill of principle. True, he went to jail only for a night. And his calm stand went unreported, save in his essay. And yet it has come down to us through the generations, a model for much that followed. We say "information" reverently, as if it meant "understanding" or "wisdom," but it doesn't. Sometimes it even gets in the way.

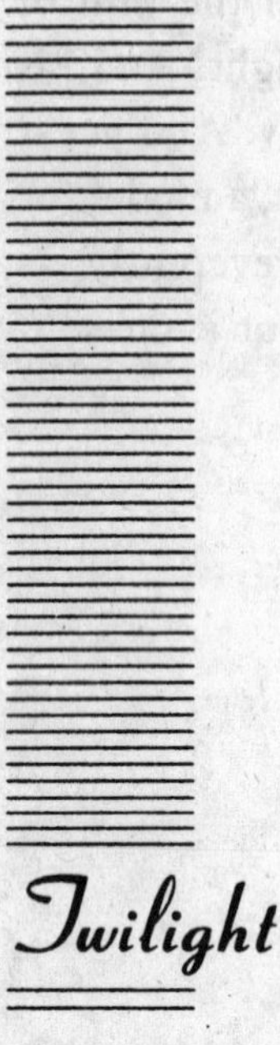

Twilight

The light lasted a long time; as it was finally fading, I saw a pickup head down the part of the road visible from the ridge. I knew, by the size of the truck and the time of the day, who it was and what he'd been doing—he'd been working on an addition for a summer house down at the lake, working late, since it was the month with no bugs, no cold, and not much dark. Not many cars drive down the road—most of them I can identify. And my sense of the community is relatively shallow. A neighbor of mine used to man a nearby fire tower for the state. From the top he could look out and see the lake where he was born and grew up, and the long unnamed ridge where he learned to hunt whitetail deer. He could see the houses of four of his eight children, and his house, or at least the valley where it sat. His mother's house, too, and the old pastures where she ran a dairy, and the church where her funeral would take place the next year, a service led by his daughter who was a sometime lay preacher there. His whole world spread out before him. He'd been to New York City exactly once, to help someone move, and somehow he'd gotten his piled-high pickup onto the bus ramp at the Port Authority bus station, and all in all it wasn't quite worth it even for a hundred dollars a day. Why leave when you're as tied in as that—when you can see a puff of smoke and know by the location and the hour if it's so-and-so burning trash or a forest fire starting up. Why leave when you live in a place you can understand and that understands you. I was putting storm windows on the church last fall with a neighbor, an older man who'd lived here all his life. He suggested we crawl up into the belfry, where I'd never been. The boards up there were covered with carved initials, most of them dating from the 1920s or earlier—some were a hundred years old. My neighbor hadn't been up there for four or five decades, but he knew whom most of the initials belonged to and whether or not they'd ended up with the female initials carved next to them. "This is my brother's," he said. "And this is mine," he added, pointing to a "DA" carved before the Depression. He pulled a knife out of his pocket and added a fresh set, complete with the initials of his wife of fifty years.

"For most of human history," writes psychologist

Paul Wachtel in his book *The Poverty of Affluence*, "people lived in tightly knit communities in which each individual had a specified place and in which there was a strong sense of shared fate. The sense of belonging, of being part of something larger than oneself, was an important source of comfort. In the face of the dangers and the terrifying mysteries that the lonely individual encountered, this sense of connectedness—along with one's religious faith, which often could hardly be separated from one's membership in the community—was for most people the main way of achieving some sense of security and the courage to go on."

"For most of human history." I have used this phrase before in this book, to try to make it clear just how different our moment is, just how much information we may be missing. In this case, the information is about "community." Many of us are used to living without strong community ties—we have friends, of course, and perhaps we're involved in the community, but we're essentially autonomous. (A 1990 survey found 72 percent of Americans didn't know their next-door neighbors.) We do our own work. We're able to pick up and move and start again. And this feels natural. It is, after all, how most modern Americans grew up. On occasion, though, we get small reminders of what a tighter community must have felt like. Camp, maybe, or senior year in high school. I can remember spring vacations when I was a teenager—the youth group from our suburban church would pile in a bus and head south for some week-long work project in a poor community. Twenty-four hours on a chartered Greyhound began to bring us together; after a week of working and eating and hanging out we had changed into a group. I can recall, too, the empty feeling when we got back to the church parking lot and our parents picked us up and we went back to the semi-isolation of suburbia—much of the fellow feeling just evaporated. I do not mean that a group of adolescents working together for a week somehow equaled a community—I do mean that there was something exhilarating about it. This twining together of lives, this intense though not always friendly communion. It seemed nearly natural. As if we were built to live that way.

"Community" is a vexed concept, of course—the ties that bind can bind too tight. Clearly, all over the world, people have felt as if they were liberating themselves when they moved to places where they could be anonymous, to the cities and suburbs that in the last seventy-five years have come to dominate the Western world. All of us have learned to luxuriate in privacy. But even just watching TV you can tell there's still a pull in the other direction, too. Fairfax Cable, on its Welcome Channel, promises you that "in our busy, fast-paced, congested world, cable TV is helping to revitalize the concept of community involvement"—in other words, they let each town in their service area operate a channel. Most of the time there is just a slow "crawl" of bulletin-board announcements, and it is from these that you can sense the desire and need for community, or at least for like-minded supportive people to whom you can turn in times of crisis. Thus there are innumerable announcements about hotlines and support groups—the child abuse hotline, the support group for mothers of AIDS patients, and so on. But in ordinary times how much community is there? The crawl of messages sheds some light on our aloneness, too. The town of Falls Church offers a service to all its elderly residents: A computer will call you at home once a day. If you don't answer, help is automatically summoned. Surely very few societies have ever needed such a thing—surely very few people lived such unaffiliated lives that their death could go unnoticed for a day.

Other functions nearly as central to the working of a community are automated too, and sold. For just ninety-five cents a minute, the 900 phone lines allow you to hear "real people" trading "confessions." That is, you can pay someone to let you gossip, or to gossip to you; eliminating communities doesn't eliminate their mild vices—it just makes them duller and costlier. New York's Channel 13, perhaps the most cerebral television channel in America, recently installed a 900 line so that people could call up after *MacNeil/Lehrer* or *Frontline* and chat with five other viewers for up to an hour—again only ninety-five cents a minute. Singles bars, once the classic symptom of modern loneliness, now involve too much contact, according to TV producer Rick Rosner; instead, you can stay at home and watch Rosner's new boy-meets-girl show, *Personals,* or maybe *Studs,* or *Love Connection,* "where old-fashioned romance meets modern technology." On May 3, a man appeared on *Love Connection* to say that the hips of the woman he had dated the night before—a lady sitting there in full view of the nation—were too large.

It's true that you can go altogether too warm and trembly at the idea of community solidarity. (The actor

Alec Baldwin, for instance, told *Hollywood Insider* how "refreshing" he had found the three days he spent in prison while researching his role in a film called *Miami Blues.* "A lot of the guys in the joint lift weights and stuff," he said. "I don't like to do that, and the other option was a lot of them box. It was the best workout I ever had. There's no cruising girls at the juice bar and all that other health club crap.") The idea that, say, small towns hum with peace and good cheer is nonsense—both *Good Morning America* and *Larry King Live* featured one tough mother from Crystal Falls, Michigan, who had gone undercover for the local cops and busted twenty-three of her friends and neighbors for selling drugs. She was not some church lady baking pies—she was mean. (On *Larry King Live,* a man phoned in to explain that *he* would teach his kids "responsible drug use." "What are you going to do, one nostril at a time?" she asked.) She left for the big city because her small-town neighbors were threatening to kill her kids.

Still, TV clearly understands that at least the *idea* of community ties attracts us. What is *Cheers* but an enclosed neighborhood where people depend on one another when the chips are down? "Where everybody knows your name. And they're always glad you came." No one moves away, no one can break up the kind of love that constantly makes jokes to keep from acknowledging that it is a kind of love. "You want to go where everybody knows your name." That's right—we do. That's why we loved *M*A*S*H,* another great TV community. But on TV, of course, while *you* know everybody's name, they've never heard of yours.

There were two Cosby episodes on this day, and both

exploited this yearning. On the rerun, his former basketball coach returned to tell stories of Cliff as a youth; in the evening, it was his great-great-aunt, an ancient but vivacious lady who had taught the children of ex-slaves to read in a one-room schoolhouse. "Many of the kids had to walk twelve miles. And when they went home they had to work their farms till sundown." She told stories of the good old days, of courting, of chaperones—of community. The program ended in church, with Mavis Staples singing a booming gospel number: "People, we all have to come together, 'cuz we need the strength and the power." It's a tribute to ties, to history—a meaningless tribute, of course, because it's all in the past tense and the present Cosbys need no one to help them lead their lives of muffled, appliance-swaddled affluence. The great-great-aunt represents a different, more primitive species, one that TV helped us "evolve" away from. But the sticky sentiment obviously plucks some strings in our hearts.

For every Hallmark card it mails to the idea of community, though, TV sends ten telegrams with the opposite meaning. Thinking of living in the same place your whole life, or even for a good long stretch of time? "No one said moving was easy. But Moving Means Moving Ahead," Allied Van Lines declares. When you reach your new home, of course, the TV will provide continuity—the same shows at the same times. And TV, of course, can provide you with people to be interested in, to gossip about—people you can take with you when you move. Not just TV actors but real-life people, like the Trumps. An interesting episode of *Donahue* focused on gossips—he interviewed a woman who ceaselessly peeked out windows to find out what her neighbors were doing. The crowd was hostile—"Get a life," one lady shouted. But all day long the same demographic group that watches *Donahue* was watching, say, *Nine Broadcast Plaza*, where an "audiologist" and a "body language analyst" analyzed the videotape of an interview that Diane Sawyer had conducted the day before with Marla Maples, the other woman in the Trump divorce. On the tape, Marla grew flustered and inarticulate when asked "Was it the best sex you ever had?" The audiologist, despite "two independent scientific instruments," could only classify her response as "inaudible," but the body language analyst thought she may have had better sex with someone else. Did she love Trump? Yes, the audiologist declared—definitely. "I don't think she knows what love is—she's too young," said the body language expert, who added that Maples was "lying through her teeth" when she said she didn't take cash from Donald. (*Nine Broadcast Plaza* also devoted time to a claim from Jessica Hahn that her encounter with Jim Bakker involved "the *worst* sex I ever had.") That night on ABC, Sam Donaldson grilled Mr. Trump himself—he refused to talk about Marla or Ivana, but did say that his yacht was "the greatest yacht in the world," and that while he bought it for $24 million, he could *easily* sell it for $115 million. Who needs eccentric uncles or town characters when you've got the Trumps?

TV's real comment on community, though, is slyer and more potent than the ones I've described so far. Day after day on sitcom after talk show after cartoon after drama, TV actively participates in the savaging of an old order it once helped set in stone. TV history, as I've said, goes back forty years. At its dawn are the shows like *Ozzie and Harriet,* synonyms for the way things were. Every day we can watch Ozzie and Harriet and Beaver and the 1950s. They represent a certain sort of community. It is no longer a physical community, really—it's faceless suburbia. But there is still some sense of shared values, albeit white and patriarchal and square and repressive values, values largely worthy of being overthrown. And TV joined gleefully in this overthrow. Every day, over and over, we relive the vanquishing of that order in the name of self-expression and human liberation and fun. The greatest story of the TV age is the transition from the fifties to the sixties—the demolition of the last ordered American "way of life." And TV tells us this story incessantly.

It begins by repeating the old shows, and therefore the old verities. On *Father Knows Best,* Bud is trying out for the football team. To win the notice of the coach, he decides to date his daughter, a sweet and innocent girl. He makes the team—but of course he doesn't feel right, so he talks to his dad. "You got what you wanted, but you feel you didn't get it fairly," Pop says gravely. "Now your conscience is bothering you, and you'll figure some way to straighten it out." Which he does, quitting the team and genuinely falling in love with her. That plot seems so exceptionally familiar and yet so distant—the football team as the pinnacle of boyish desire, the formal courtship of the girl complete with long talks with her father. And especially the act of going to one's own parents to talk about such matters.

It is resolutely unhip, almost as unhip as the *Leave It to Beaver* episode that begins with Eddie Haskell's attempts to cheat on a history exam (a history exam with questions on Clemenceau and Lloyd George) and ends as, reformed, he dutifully recites the first six countries to ratify the League of Nations charter.

But TV doesn't simply offer us these shows as relics—consciously and unconsciously it pokes fun at them. Consider this promo for Nick at Nite's nonstop week of *Donna Reed Show* reruns: "This is Donna Reed, supercompetent mother of two and wife of one," says the announcer, who is imitating Robin Leach. "She lives in this spectacular American dream house, which she cleans for her husband, the handsome Dr. Stone. Dinnertime at Chez Stone features meat, usually accompanied by potatoes, and takes place in this spotless dream kitchen!" Over pictures of people in gas masks and belching factories, the announcer says mockingly, "Out to save a world that's made a mess of things, she comes—mighty Hoover vacuum in hand. It's Donna Reed, sent from TV land to lead us politely into the new millennium."

Even when the ridicule is less explicit, it's fascinating to see the old order break down in front of your eyes each night. Over two hours on a single channel I watched a progression that began with Lucy trying desperately to get the handsome new teacher to ask her out on a date. Then came *That Girl!*, where Marlo Thomas was living alone in the city and faring well but still desperate for her parents to like her cooking. *Rhoda* was next—she went to the house of her husband's ex-wife to pick up the kids and they got roaring drunk. And finally, on *Phyllis,* most of the humor came from a cackling granny who loved to watch golf on TV because the golfers keep bending over and displaying their rear ends. In case you weren't getting the point, the shows were interspersed with ads like this one, for a videotape library of old TV shows: "The fifties—life seemed simpler then. Drive-ins, chrome-covered cars, and every Monday night there was *Lucy.*"

This account of our liberation from the repressive mores of society is not an entirely new story (as the Zeffirelli version of *Romeo and Juliet* on Showtime made clear), but never has it been told so ceaselessly. Steve Vai had a tune in heavy rotation this week on MTV—it showed a young boy with a prim old lady for a teacher. He jumps up on the desk to play his guitar for show-and-tell, and the kids, liberated by the beat, tear the room apart; the teacher goes screaming out into the hall. The children watching this video have likely never known this sort of school, where learning is by rote and repression is the rule. And yet this mythical liberation survives, celebrated over and over again, as it will as long as the people who lived through that revolution are writing TV shows. (And perhaps as long as the people who grew up watching those shows are writing them, and so on forever.)

Any revolution this constant and thorough breeds counterrevolt, or at least uneasiness. Sometimes it is explicit, as with the conservatives who haunt the religious channels preaching "traditional family values." Usually, though, the uneasiness creeps in around the edges. On pay-per-view, *Field of Dreams* concerned a fellow, Ray Kinsella, who was a big wheel in the antiwar movement. He retains a fair amount of contempt for the stolid farmers around him, and his wife certainly stands up against book-burning bigots. But there's also a lot in the movie about his dad, who just wanted to play catch with him. Ray rejected all that family stuff in a huff and went off to college to protest—and now, more or less, he has to build a big stadium in the cornfield in order to get his daddy back. He'd gone a little bit too far back then.

Other, lesser movies made the same kind of point. HBO ran a fascinating film, *Irreconcilable Differences,* about a little girl who was suing her parents for divorce. They had been the classic sixties couple—they met as *semihippies* on a *road trip* across America. He'd written his thesis about *sexual overtones* in *early films.* She decided to dump her *Navy fiancé.* They drank *tequila* and listened to *James Taylor* and *cried* at films. And then they got rich writing movies on their own and fulfilled themselves in all sorts of predictable ways—divorces, bimbos, personal masseuses, big houses, fast cars. They were "doing their thing," "following their bliss." Which is why their daughter ends up explaining to the judge that she wants to go live with the Mexican housekeeper in her tiny bungalow, where the children sleep three to a bed. "I don't expect my mom to be a person who vacuums all day and bakes cookies for me when I get home from school, and I don't expect my dad to be some kind of real understanding person who wants to take me fishing all the time. But my mom and dad are just too mixed up for anyone to be around. I'm just a kid, and I don't know what I'm doing sometimes. But I think you should know better when you grow up." Their reconciliation comes in a cheap chain restaurant—utter normality as salvation.

This kind of reaction, though, has not really slowed the trend away from Ozzie and Harriet. One critic described Fox's *Married . . . With Children* as "antimatter to the Huxtables. . . . Sex (both the desire for and aversion to), the body at its grossest, stupidity, and familial contempt are the stuff of this sitcom." And yet, as CBS programmer Howard Stringer pointed out ruefully, more children were watching the program than any show on CBS. Therefore, he said, he was sending a signal to producers of comedy shows that they had an "open throttle" to change the network's image as "stuffy, stodgy, and old." He pointed with pride to an upcoming CBS pilot show that, in the words of the *Times,* "contains a provocative line of dialogue from a six-year-old girl." On *Leave It to Beaver,* Ricky talks to his girlfriend on the phone in the living room in front of his parents and thinks nothing of it. By the *Brady Bunch,* the girls are giggling secretly over the princess phone. When you get to *One Day at a Time,* the children listen in as the mother talks to *her* boyfriend, who's trying to persuade her to come to a South Pacific island. "He's probably down there starving for your body, lusting for your lips," the daughter says. And *One Day at a Time* is already in reruns.

Ozzie and Harriet represented all sorts of things that needed to be overthrown, or at least badly shaken up—a world where women did what housework remained, where children never talked back, where appearance and conformity counted above all, where black people never showed their faces, where sex was dirty or absent, where

God lived in some church, where America was the only country that counted. The problem is only that the rebellion against this world never ended, never helped create a new and better order to take its place. The American Revolution tossed out the tyrants and set up something fresh; the French Revolution tossed out tyrants and then looked for more tyrants.

The main idea that emerges from the breakup of this Donna Reed order is "freedom," or, more accurately, not being told what to do. You can listen to, say, sociologist Robert Bellah when he says "personal freedom, autonomy, and independence are the highest values for Americans," or you can listen to the crowd on one of the morning talk shows responding to the plight of a man whose XXXtasy hardcore pornography television service has been shut down by an Alabama sheriff. "It's just total censorship," someone in the studio audience said. "It all comes down to the same thing—our rights." "Everyone out there has to make their own decisions." The same kind of sentiments attended the 2 Live Crew controversy, which came to a head while I was working on this book. The Crew, you will recall, was the rap group that specialized in lyrics like "Suck my dick, bitch, and make it puke," and which finally found one cooperative Florida district attorney who rose to the bait and charged them with obscenity. As Sara Rimer reported in the *Times,* Luther Campbell, the group's leader, said he was worried that the six jurors, who included three women over age sixty and only one black, might be "too old, too white, and too middle-class" to "understand" his music. His worry was misplaced; after they quickly acquitted him, one juror said, "I thought it would've been cute if we could of come out with the verdict like we were doing a rap song," and another said the content of the lyrics had not affected her: "Those were their songs. They were doing their poetry in song."

The jurors made the right decision—"You take away one freedom and pretty soon they're all gone," said one, and he was telling the truth. So were the people on *Nine Broadcast Plaza*—an Alabama sheriff shouldn't care what folks watch on their TVs. Tolerance is an unqualified good—a world where people of all races and all sexual orientations and both genders and all political persuasions can express themselves openly is so manifestly superior to the bigoted and repressed world we're leaving behind that they hardly bear comparison. And it's probably even useful to have occasional phenomena like 2 Live Crew to make us stand up once again and reassert our principles.

But tolerance by itself can be a cover for moral laziness. In a world with real and pressing problems, tolerance is merely a precondition for politics—it is not itself a meaningful politics. We try to pretend that "liberation" is enough because it's so much easier to eternally rebel: "Kicking against social repression and moral vapidity—that's an activity rock 'n' roll has managed to do better than virtually any other art or entertainment form," *Rolling Stone* boasted in a year-end editorial in 1990 that called for forming a "bulwark against those who would gladly muzzle that spirit . . . of insolent liberty." Good, fine, we all agree—"I thought it would've been cute if we could of come out with the verdict like we were doing a rap song."

But is that all there is? Don't popular music and art and politics have a good deal more to do than "kick against social repression and moral vapidity"? Isn't it time to focus harder on substantive problems, such as, how do we build a society that doesn't destroy the planet by its greed, and doesn't *ignore* the weak and poor? (Not repress them, just ignore them.) I don't mean a lot of sappy records and TV shows with syrupy messages about saving dolphins—I mean popular art that fulfills the old functions of popular art, that reminds us of our connections with one another and with the places we live. An art that reminds us that our own lives shouldn't merely be free—that they should be of value to others, connected to others, and that if our lives are like that they will become finer. That's what a culture is. It's true that we don't need all the old "traditional" values—but as a society we desperately need *values.*

We need them because a culture primarily obsessed with "tolerance" as an end instead of a means is, finally, a selfish culture, a have-it-your-way world. A place where nothing interferes with desire, the definition of a perfect consumer society. Listen to Jerry Della Femina, the adman, on *Good Morning America.* He's excoriating Disney for not letting movie theaters show commercials with its films: "Disney is blackmailing the movie theaters. . . . It should be up to the audience. If you hate the commercial, boo and hiss. If you like the commercial, buy the product. That's the American way." Or listen to Marion Barry, who in 1990 was still the mayor of Washington but had already been indicted on any number of drug and malfeasance charges. The city Democratic committee was voting that night on a motion urging him not to run for reelection. "It amounts to a type of censorship," he told one network. "Our country was founded on the principle that all men have a right to life, liberty, and the pursuit of happiness. And I intend to pursue my happiness as I see fit." By the late news, he's Daniel Webster—"I'd rather die losing and stand on principle." The principle is that no one should tell him what to do, never mind that his city was a grotesque shambles. That night, a woman stood up at the Democratic meeting to defend Barry: "We're not Hitler, and we can't say who should run and who should not run." This is tolerance replacing sense.

Though it's rarely mentioned on TV, the gay community in the wake of the AIDS crisis provides an alternative example. Randy Shilts's eloquent history of the crisis, *And the Band Played On*, begins in San Francisco, where gay people had carved out an enclave of freedom and tolerance in a hostile world. And then, out of nowhere, not as a punishment but as a fact, came a strange disease. It was a proud community, and a community tolerant, even indulgent, of all desires. The emerging understanding of the disease—that it was sexually transmitted, that safety lay in limiting both partners and practices—conflicted sharply with that tolerant ethos. Some people said that closing the bathhouses or educating people about what not to stick where would force people back into the closet, interfere with their freedom, return them to the repressed past. But AIDS was a fact. Gradually—a little too gradually, probably—the gay community came as a group to embrace other values, to form a community that in its organized compassion, active caring, and political toughness is a model for every other community in America. A mature community. This does not mean that AIDS was a good thing. Far, far better it had never come, and life had gone on as before, and none of those tens of thousands had died. But AIDS was and is a fact, a shocking enough fact to force people into changing, into realizing that along with tolerance and liberation they now need commitment and selflessness.

By accepting the idea that we should never limit desire or choose from the options our material and spiritual liberations give us, we ignore similarly pressing facts about our larger community. In a different world perhaps we'd never need to limit our intake of goods, to slow down our consumption of resources, to stop and share with others. But we live in this world—a world approaching ecological disaster, riven by poverty. A world of limits, demanding choices. TV gives us infinite information about choice—it celebrates choice as a great blessing, which it is, and over the course of a single day it lays out a nearly infinite smorgasbord of options. As much as it loves choice, though, it doesn't actually believe in choosing. It urges us to choose *everything*—this and this and this as well. And it does nothing to help us create the communities that might make wise choices possible on a scale large enough to make a difference.

In this case, the mountain is useful mostly as a vantage point. It can offer scant advice about how humans should organize their lives together, but it does provide an aerial view; from up here on the ridge I can recognize each home by its kitchen lights, and see how they stand in relation to one another. And now the all-night light has switched on at the volunteer fire department, whose noon siren was about the only mechanical sound I heard all day.

No need, as I said, to romanticize small towns—they can be home to vicious feud and rankling gossip and small-minded prejudice and all the other things that made leaving them appear so liberating. But there are a few things to be said for them, and the volunteer fire department is one. A house fire is no joke—when you take the state qualifying course, they show you film after film of houses exploding with folks inside, just as in *Backdraft.* On this day, in fact, the Washington TV stations were covering a tragedy in a tiny Pennsylvania village, Hustontown. The firemen had been called to clean out a well for an old lady. It smelled funny, but they thought there was just a dead animal down there. The first man down suddenly lost consciousness—two more jumped down to get him. All three died from some gas that had collected there. The fiancée of one of the men sobbed hysterically on the porch of a nearby house—she'd begged him not to go, but "he told me it was his duty as a volunteer firefighter." His duty, that is, to friends, neighbors, community.

It may be more sensible, by some utilitarian calculation, to entrust your safety to trained professionals and to insurance companies—more reliable, perhaps, and in places of a certain size clearly necessary. But it comes at a cost in information. Abstracted from others, you begin to believe in your own independence, forgetting that at some level you depend on everyone else and they depend on you, even if it's only to pay taxes. (Pretty soon you don't want to pay taxes anymore.) "We place a high value on being left alone, on not being interfered with," says Bellah, the sociologist who has interviewed hundreds of Americans. "The most important thing is to be able to take care of yourself. . . . It's illegitimate to depend on another human being." And this belief is so lonely—it's something human beings have never had to contend with before.

Public television was airing a Bill Moyers interview with a businessman named James Autry. A former brand manager for Colgate, he was trained at Benton & Bowles advertising agency and now worked as the publisher of *Better Homes & Gardens.* He is also a poet. He took Moyers back to the Mississippi town where he'd grown up—where his father, Reverend Autry, had spent his life preaching at the local church in the piney woods. The son had left the South in part to escape its ugly, intolerant side—he didn't want all that went with being a white Southerner. But he'd started coming back in recent years—he sat in the graveyard next to his daddy's church and read a poem: "She was a McKinstry, and his mother was a Smith / And the listeners nod at what that combination will produce / Those generations to come of honesty or thievery / Of heathens or Christians / Of slovenly men or worthy. / Course his mother was a Sprayberry. . . ." And he said, this man who publishes *Better Homes & Gardens,* which convinces millions that a better home is a home with better furniture, "I've thought about my own sons. What are they connected to? Some house on Fifty-sixth Street in Des Moines? What will they remember?" And this is a hard and terrible question for all of us who grew up liberated.

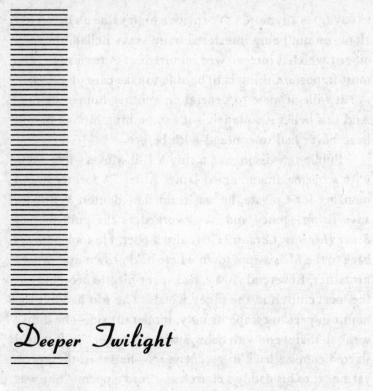

Deeper Twilight

Time for a swim. I ease myself down from the rocks into the chilly water, feeling the mud between my toes. I stand for a minute, aware of the line on my calves between the cold of water and the warmth of sun, and then dive in a taut stretch. I can feel the water rushing past my head, smoothing back my hair. As I stroke out to the middle, I'm conscious of the strength and pull of my shoulder blades. I haul myself out onto a rock in the middle of the pond, and sit there dripping. A breeze comes up, and lifts the hairs on my back, each one giving a nearly imperceptible tug at my skin. Under hand and thigh I can feel the roughness and the hardness of the rock. If I listen, I can hear the birds singing from several trees around the shore, and a frog now and again, and from the outlet stream a few hundred yards away a faint burbling—always changing and always the same. If I listen without concentrating, it's mainly the wind that I hear, a steady slight pressure on the leaves. I can see a hundred things—the sun reflects off the ripples from my passage and casts a moving line of shadow and sparkle on the rocks that rise up at the water's edge. I can smell the water. I can taste the water too—not the neutral beverage you drink because there's nothing in the fridge, but wet, rich, *complete.* As it drops into the corner of my mouth there's the slightest tang of salt from the trail sweat of the afternoon. I can feel my weight—feel it disappear as I slip into the water, feel it cling to me again as I drag myself back onto the rock.

TV restricts the use of our senses—that's one of the ways it robs us of information. It asks us to use our eyes and ears, and only our eyes and ears. If it is doing its job "correctly," you lose consciousness of your body, at least until a sort of achy torpor begins to assert itself, and maybe after some hours a dull headache, and of course the insatiable hunger that you never really notice but that somehow demands a constant stream of chips and soda. If you cut off your nose to spite your face, or for any other reason, it wouldn't impair your ability to watch television. You could make these same objections about other mediums, too—about writing, maybe. You can't smell words on a page. But you can summon a sense of smell. I hope the first paragraph of this chapter, however dimly, triggered your sense memory; it is not, I think, reproducible on television.

Even the senses that TV caters to, sight and hearing, it limits. It rarely provides a vista, not unless the Goodyear blimp is on hand. (My family gathered around the TV each New Year's Day for the opening seconds of the Rose Bowl coverage because the camera would briefly pan around the Los Angeles mountains where we once lived.) Its instinct is for the close-up. In the three or four years between the time I stopped watching TV and the time I began this project, the camera had tightened in dramatically on people's faces, especially during commercials—a man would be selling you financial services and you could count the worry lines around his eyes. But this tight shot demands one center of attention. If you're shooting *Nova,* you can get a nifty shot of an ant mating, but you can't, say, lie on your stomach and observe one square foot of ground. Here's a big spidery thing waving back and forth on improbable legs, and a line of ants, and the wind dropping needles from the bottom bough of a small pine. TV can't deal with faint noise, either; even "background" music is in the foreground, and only one sound at a time is permitted. When people shout, the decibel level doesn't really rise much—you knew Crazy Eddie was screaming because of his hand gestures, not his volume, which was certainly a blessing, but it all contributes to the sense of living in a muffled, shrunken world.

TV chops away perspective, too. On the mountain, even if your eye is drawn to something in particular, your peripheral vision fills in all sorts of detail, constantly. When you watch TV your peripheral vision ceases to function—you stare at the screen like a pitcher staring in at the catcher's mitt. You no longer even notice the *set*—the frame, the knobs, the antenna (if you're still backward enough to need an antenna). Your vision is cut down to maybe 10 degrees of the horizon—on a large screen maybe 15 degrees. What we see, we see sharply—the images have been edited so that peripheral vision is unnecessary. In the Cosby living room there is a staircase, and in front of it a sofa, and the family is sitting on the sofa. No one is off in the corner making faces—it's fantastically stripped down, uncomplicated, and as a consequence whoever is in the foreground assumes vaster importance than he'd be granted under an open sky.

Any art, of course, does this to one degree or another—the artist wants you to focus on something she has chosen, picked out from the world. But the experience of watching, say, a play in the theater differs vastly from the experience of watching a television drama. The curtain comes up and down, lights shift on and off, the volume goes up and down—if you are sitting front row left you may see action quite different from what you would fifteen seats to the right or thirty behind. Most of all, you can *choose* what to watch. There is more there than the eye can take in, far more. You may spend the whole scene looking at what the TV director would call the reaction shot, or you may let yourself get caught up in the background. Sometimes the actors come right out among you—they may touch you. In any case, your absorption is of an entirely different character. Movies move in the direction of television, but even they have much more periphery—even on HDTV with Dolby stereo it's hard to imagine a television epic, a spectacle. No one's ever shot a scene for television with a cast of thousands.

Or consider the difference between watching a baseball game on TV and watching one at the park. Technology enriches the TV version with close-up and slo-mo and instant replay, but at a great price. It deprives you of the enormous perspective available to anyone in the stadium, the incredible choice of what to look at. TV looks at pretty women on occasion but never at the fight in the stands or the man selling beer or the outfielder hitching his pants. TV filters out most of the familiar sound of the ballpark, too—the sourceless, undifferentiated babble that comes from forty thousand people talking, laughing, rustling sacks of popcorn, a sound that the crack of the bat breaks so cleanly through, refocusing everyone's attention. TV systems are planning to introduce new interactive technology that will allow you to select between, say, three or four camera angles during the course of a game. But this sort of choice only underlines how much TV amputates your senses. What is there at a circus that can't be topped by a hundred spectacles a night on television? And yet circuses survive—what TV picture can compete with the humid excitement? And three rings! A delicious overload of the senses, starved on television's visual Pritikin regimen. Still, the time may be coming when this overload seems like too much—when we prefer our baseball on TV. When it begins to seem more *real* on TV. At the beginning of *And So*

It Goes, Linda Ellerbee's book about her TV career, she recalls a conversation with colleagues about whether her new show should be live or on tape. Her son Josh overheard the argument and interrupted: "This is live," he said. "You, me, everybody in this room. *This* is live. That, Mom," he said pointing to the box, "*that's* television."

During the war in the Persian Gulf, people said we were seeing things as they happened, live, with gut-wrenching immediacy. In truth, we were seeing what television was able to show us—the lights of tracer fire flashing over Baghdad were in some way impressive, but if I'd been told they were a laser show commemorating the hundredth anniversary of the Iraqi electric utility I'd have nodded my head. The shudder, the concussion, the dust, the smell, all the things that even a moderately competent writer would express, TV can't. Most of all, the confusion—the camera and the small screen can't cope with confusion because they search relentlessly for a center, a focus. "Does TV 'bring the war into your living room'?" asked Mark Crispin Miller in his book *Boxed-In.* "In fact, the experience is fundamentally absurd. Most obviously there is an incongruity of scale, the radical disjunction of locations. While a war is among the biggest things that can ever happen to a nation or a person, devastating families, blasting away the roofs and walls, we see it compressed and miniaturized on a sturdy little piece of furniture, which stands and shines at the very center of our household." If you wanted even the slightest sense of what the war in Iraq was *like,* how it *felt,* you'd be far better off hiring someone to come at some random hour in the night and toss a brick through your window.

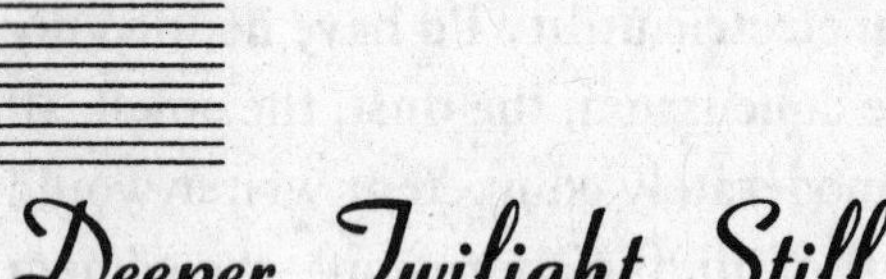

Deeper Twilight Still

I've been sitting on a flat rock next to the pond for many minutes, watching the sun go down and seeing the stars come up. When I got out of the water, I drip-dried in the last sun—the stored soft heat in the rock warmed my back. I sat there without a shirt on, for the breeze kept down the few mosquitoes. The air grew cooler and cooler—the breeze felt great, and then right on the line between great and chilly, and then just plain cool till it raised gooseflesh, but I was too happy with the stars to move. Finally I got up, and wandered back to the tent, dug out a clean T-shirt, and pulled it over my head—and thought about how great it felt. How dry against the back of my neck where my wet hair still dripped, how warm against the breeze, how soft compared with the rock I'd been lying on. It occurs to me that I may have cast myself as a killjoy in this book, an antimaterialist, the unsensual man, but it isn't true. The mountain is filled with deep animal satisfaction—far better stocked with physical pleasure than any fancy home or leather-lined car. That's because the mountain also exposes you to cold, damp, wind, heat—when you finish with these and move on to warm, dry, still, cool, you feel not just comfort. You feel *pleasure, joy.*

The difference between comfort and pleasure is enormous, though hard to set down in words. Albert Borgmann says "comfort is the feeling of well-being that derives from an optimally high and steady level of arousal of positive stimulation, whereas pleasure arises from an upward change of the arousal level. Since there is a best or highest level of pleasure that constitutes comfort, one cannot indefinitely obtain pleasure by rising from comfort to more comfort. . . . Hence pleasure can only be had at the price of discomfort." What he means, I think, is, if you walk out of the bitter cold into a 70-degree room, it will feel *marvelous, toasty, cheerful, a haven, a nest.* But if you spend all your time in a room where the temperature is 70 degrees it will simply feel neutral. I can remember my father talking about taking a long hiking trip around Mount Rainier. At the end of the trek, after days of water and the kind of food you carry with you on a trail, he emerged, went to a restaurant, and ordered a milk shake. And I think he can taste that milk shake still—whereas, of course, if you have a milk shake every day you hardly notice it. This is the most obvious thing on earth, and yet it is the easiest to forget. When you are sitting inside on a cold and windy night it is nearly impossible to make yourself get up and walk the dog, even though when you do, the fresh air feels bracing, and the home you return to is a magic place.

The great virtue of the mountain is that once you're up there away from the car, there's no way to escape those kinds of swings—the information about what actually feels good is forced on you relentlessly. The second day I was up there it rained like crazy—little rivers finding the stitching holes in my old tent. It stopped for a while in the morning and I went out for a short hike—ten minutes from the tent the clouds opened up again, and by the time I was back you could have wrung me out. Nothing to do but crawl into my damp sleeping bag and read. It was too hot inside the sleeping bag and my legs sweated. Outside the bag was too cool—clammy. And then, in the afternoon, the sun broke through, the rain fled, the world warmed up. I stretched out my gear and myself on a rock and warmed up—and that sun felt ten times as glorious because of the rain that came before it.

We are stubbornly unwilling to acknowledge this kind of pleasure—either that or we habitually overstate the discomfort that precedes it. On the *Today* show, Bryant Gumbel announced that in a few weeks the whole cast was going on a camping trip so they could broadcast from the great outdoors. Co-host Deborah Norville shrieked girlishly: "We're not sleeping in tents, are we?" When Bryant said yes, she said, "The heck we are. . . . There's nothing in my contract that says I have to sleep in tents. I feel an illness coming on—exactly what date is that? Oooooh, crawly things," and so on.

If this were simply a physical phenomenon, it would be bad enough—a loss of information about our bodies that has enriched the lives of most members of every previous generation, and a loss of understanding about what it is is like for others to be cold and hungry and dirty. But it's more than that. We have developed a series of emotional thermostats as well, by far the most potent of which is television itself. Instead of really experiencing the highs and lows, pain and joys, that make up a life, many of us use TV just as we use central heating—to flatten our variations, to maintain a constant "optimal" temperature. A pair of academics, Robert Kubey and Mihaly Cziksentmihalyi, recently published a massive and novel study of why people watch TV. Instead of assembling their subjects in a college classroom somewhere, showing them a program, and passing out questionnaires, Kubey and Cziksentmihalyi tried to find out what TV meant to people in the ordinary course of life. Each subject was given a beeper, which went off eight or nine times a day at random intervals between 8:00 A.M. and 10:00 P.M. When the pager sounded, the subjects were supposed to instantly fill out a form that showed what they were doing at the time and how they were feeling—whether they were concentrating, what kind of mood they were in, if their head was aching, whether they really wished they were doing something else.

Some of the findings were obvious: "Television is used by some singles in lieu of company when dining." But much of their research broke new ground. Their data showed quite convincingly that people watch television when they felt depressed—that the strongest variable predicting that people would watch TV in the evening was that in the afternoon they felt the day was going badly. Only a minority, described as "rare" in one study, watch television "selectively," in order to see a few favorite shows—only about half of Americans report even using a television guide. Instead, we use the set like a drug. Not an addictive drug exactly—the idea that people are addicted to TV has a long history, and surely all of us have sometimes felt it to be true. But the new research indicates that it's not a drug like crack—that watching it actually makes us feel more passive, bored, irritable, sad, and lonely. There was certainly no euphoria, not even much active pleasure. TV didn't dominate people's thoughts all day—when they were beeped at work, in only five of three thousand cases were people thinking about programs. If our lives are going pleasantly, if there's something else to do that's attractive, even if it's as undramatic as chatting on the phone with friends, then we're much less likely to watch TV. We use TV as we use tranquilizers—to even things out, to blot out unpleasantness, to dilute confusion, distress, unhappiness, loneliness. The reason that television can be counted on to work this way—the way that television most nearly resembles a drug—is its predictability. It is *not* a drug like LSD; you don't take it to see where you'll be transported to today. You take it because you *know* where you'll be transported. *General Hospital* can be counted on to rouse the same emotions at the same time each day, as can *Jeopardy* or *Nightline* or *Letterman.* In an uncertain world, TV restores an old familiar pattern. The Corporation for Public Broadcasting once commissioned a study to discover why people weren't flocking to its "innovative" programming. It found people preferred commercial TV precisely *because* on the networks they were "more likely to see familiar actors and episodes of programs they had viewed previously." When Rhoda separated from her TV husband the ratings dropped; when *M*A*S*H* killed off McLean Stevenson, it drew bagloads of angry mail.

That's one reason the *Playhouse 90*–type programs that originally dominated TV have fallen by the wayside—you wouldn't know, from one night to the next, if you were going to be scared or shocked or amused. It's why all those people who called Walter Cronkite the most influential man in America were wrong. He held our affection because he was utterly predictable, right down to his inflection, and had he suddenly urged us to rise up and break our chains he would instantly have gone from soothing to alarming—he would have broken the trance we turn on television to create.

This tranquilization has its advantages—anyone who ever checked into a hotel room knows that TV masks the loneliness. And if it really made us happy, who could argue? Loneliness, stress, fear—these aren't to be desired, exactly. But television doesn't leave us happy; it only presses our boredom and alienation a little to the back. "Obviously," wrote Kubey and Cziksentmihalyi, "if they possibly could, TV producers would regularly broadcast programs that would make people feel significantly happier than they do normally. They would do so because of the obvious commercial gains that would accrue. That television viewing helps us feel more relaxed than usual but generally does not help us feel substantially happier says something about human nature and what makes for happiness. Happiness is a more complex state than relaxation. It requires a more elusive set of conditions, and is therefore more difficult to obtain. Others can successfully attract and hold our attention and help us relax, but perhaps only we can provide for ourselves the psychological rewards and meaning that make for happiness." In the same way that traveling by airline assures your comfort but rarely allows you any adventure along the way, watching TV insulates you from anything real. We all know this—when researchers ask what activity best fits the description "I should have been doing something else," television is the hands-down winner. But that something else might be unpleasant—it might mean dealing with a spouse you'd rather not deal with, or thinking about a job that leaves you empty and unfulfilled. Or that something else might be risky—television never even thinks about rejecting you. Under the pressure of your thumb it comes instantly to life, cooing and making eyes.

That's why TV makes us feel so guilty sometimes. It's a time-out from life. Which is okay if you're really winded—TV as white-noise therapy has its occasional value. But the time-outs soon last longer than the game, which at some level you realize is passing you by. TV makes it so easy to postpone living for another half hour. I can remember hundreds of Saturday afternoons as a boy spent staring at *Wide World of Sports.* I wasn't much of an athlete then—a deep fear of embarrassment kept me out of Pop Warner and Little League. So I lay on the sofa and watched cliff diving in Acapulco and learned to mildly loathe myself.

I've taken friends up the mountain to the pond many times, and at the top suggested a swim. Invariably some of them hang back—it's too cold, or they don't want anyone to think they're fat, or they'd be soggy on the hike down, or all the other inhibitions we feel in such situations. But you can tell, when everyone else is whooping and hollering in the frigid water, that they wish they'd come in.

9:00 P.M.

On *Twin Peaks,* Agent Cooper goes to the vet to track down the bird that attacked Laura Palmer, and finds a llama in the waiting room. The Indian deputy reveals that his girlfriend got her PhD from Brandeis. Two girls stand in the high school bathroom talking about Laura—one says the idea that she worked in a brothel gives her "a hot, cold" feeling, "like when you hold an ice cube on your bare skin for a long time." Another young woman, this one with her blouse open, rubs herself with a loaded handgun. The search continues for the one-armed man. It's hard to remember now that it's gone off the air, but for a brief moment in the spring of 1990 *Twin Peaks* was seen as vitally important, as culture come to the small screen, as "quality," as the future—everyone talked endlessly about David Lynch's marvelous *sensibility.* "In this country TV is used primarily as a narcotic to prepare people for the commercial," said Lynch's co-creator, Mark Frost. "As we've just seen in Eastern Europe, it can also be an instrument for social change. We created a show that we'd like people to watch. It undercuts people's expectations and asks them to pay attention. Anything that makes people more alert is positive."

Whether or not *Twin Peaks* was a "good show" is beside the point. *Twin Peaks* was just one in a line of breakthroughs. Quite regularly, every two or three seasons, a program emerges that is going to change TV, to point the way forward. It's as if everyone agrees that TV is pretty shabby, but hopes and trusts that it's about to get great, to start enlightening us. To become "an instrument for social change." To educate our young. To open up new worlds, new attitudes. The particular show either goes off the air because no one watches it or settles into a rut (by the fall of 1990, the TV critic for *Rolling Stone* was referring to *Twin Peaks* as *Freaky Dynasty*). It may leave stylistic tracks; it may "break new ground" with its "frankness" (that is, the amount of innuendo or skin); it may spawn spinoffs and imitations—but it's over.

Soon, though, like an ex-boyfriend, television's back at the door with roses and candy. "Look, I know I was a jerk. But this time it'll be different. I've changed. From now on I'm going to be clever, creative. I'm going to be like Jackie

Gleason." But pretty soon, of course, its skin is splitting and turning green—it's forgotten all its promises and turned back into *The Incredible Hulk.* (Following up on *its* refreshing breakthrough show *The Simpsons,* the Fox network premiered its new programs a little early in the fall of 1990. The one they were really plugging was called *Babes,* the story of three sisters whose gimmick was chronic, severe, and ostensibly hilarious obesity.)

Many people have a defensible, simple, and even noble reason for believing that TV will improve—TV's audience is so vast that anyone who hopes for a different future, a more enlightened nation, wants to borrow its demographic power. On Bravo, Gabriel García Márquez told an interviewer he was going to make a soap opera for Colombian TV. "I am drawn to it like a magnetic pole," he said. "The medium has to be used. It is an invitation to a truly spectacular dissemination of one's thoughts."

This hope is as old as TV. Listen to the Ford Foundation in 1961: "Students in today's classrooms can be eyewitnesses to history in the making. . . . They can see and hear the outstanding scholars of our age. They can have access to the great museums of art, history, and nature. A whole treasure-trove of new and stimulating experiences that were beyond the reach of yesterday's students can be brought into the classroom for today's students." Or the Carnegie Commission on Educational Television in 1967 (a panel that included Rudolf Serkin, James Conant, Ralph Ellison, and Edwin Land): "Television has been fashioned into a miraculous instrument. . . . What confronts our society is the obligation to bring that technology into the full service of man, so that its power to move image and sound is consistently coupled with a power to move mind and spirit. . . . The utilization of a great technology for great purposes, the appeal to excellence in the service of diversity—these finally became the concepts that gave shape to the work of the commission." Or, twelve years later, in 1979, the next Carnegie panel, this one including Bill Moyers, Alex Haley, and Walter Heller: Broadcasting can "help the creative spirit to flourish. It can reveal how we are different and what we share in common. It can illuminate the dark corners of the world and the dark corners of the mind. . . . It can delight us. It can entertain us. It can inform us. Above all, it can add to our understanding of our own inner workings and of one another."

This sense of unrealized potential continues right to the present. The *UTNE Reader*, a digest of progressive writing from small magazines, recently devoted an issue to "Re-Thinking TV—Is It Time to Turn On, Tune In, and Take Charge?" Its essayists urged that every public school "be equipped with closed-circuit audio and video systems and studio facilities . . . to give every child adequate hands-on experience," and that "weekly or monthly electronic town meetings" be held in major cities across the nation so that "a new level of communication and accountability could be established between the public and decision-makers." Some writers thought there should be mandated numbers of foreign films, or "sports from Borneo and Mali," or "world-beat soaps." Even if that doesn't happen, wrote a professor, schools can teach their students to "deconstruct" programs like *Family Ties*—"with the advent of such devices as videocassettes and camcorders, people are busy constructing their own realities, which in itself may have social and political implications. It makes your head spin."

Indeed it does—it always has and always will. TV is like a mighty river surrounded by eager civil engineers. Surely society must be able to harness a force this powerful, and with it move worlds. But is it ever going to happen? At the moment, environmentalists are hardest at work in Hollywood planting messages in the scripts of films and TV shows. "Historically it is the artist who leads," says Tom Cruise, a backer of the newly formed Earth Communications Office, and so in *Lethal Weapon 2*, Danny Glover's family enlightens Mel Gibson about how dolphins get killed in tuna nets. On *Knots Landing,* a baby-faced psycho security guard is about to murder the hostess of a TV talk show. That's the plot, but, in passing, the fictional show's producer stops the hostess in the hall and says, "This is the book I was telling you about—*Fifty Simple Things You Can Do to Save the Earth.* I think it has a lot of great topic ideas for the show." And the viewer is supposed to buy the book someday, or at least think that saving the earth is a glamorous idea.

Plenty of other people want to use the technology more directly, not by inserting their cause into sitcoms but by stating it outright. Tony Schwartz, the adman who did the famous mushroom-cloud spots for LBJ, and who once wrote a book called *Media: The Second God,* recently announced the formation of a Media Peace Corps to help educate the public about important issues. For instance, he told the *Times,* "They don't have enough money for restaurant inspectors in New York, but we could do commercials telling people how to check restaurants for code violations." Though the image of thousands of New York diners touring the kitchens to check out dishwasher temperatures is too delightful for words, I have my doubts.

The fondest hope of all, repeatedly dashed but never destroyed, is that TV can be harnessed to educate children. By the time I reached grade school, the library had already been converted to an Instructional Materials Center, crowded with TVs and viewers and so on—eventually, a lot of people assumed, most instruction would come from a set. This vision has not faded altogether—*Newsweek* recently reported on a current events teacher at a good South Carolina high school who tapes the news for his current events classes. "In one recent class," the magazine said, the teacher "periodically stopped the VCR so that students could discuss the coverage. . . . 'What's Imelda Marcos famous for?' he asked during a segment on her upcoming trial. 'Shoes,' the class yelled back. 'Who does that remind you of?' the teacher prompted. 'Tammy Faye Bakker,' the students shot back." And on the Fairfax system, several channels belong to school systems and colleges—one teacher was gamely offering Latin II over the air. It seemed exactly like most other Latin classes, except that kids kept phoning in with wonderful excuses ("We wanted to call and ask you about your quiz today, because the cable was down on Wednesday, and we didn't get good reception yesterday at all"). It seemed like a relic, actually—like a Picturephone, something from the past, not the future. This bloom was wilted—the outcry over Channel One, a competent ten-minute news show aimed at schoolkids and interrupted with candy commercials, makes the old vision of an electronic classroom seem remote.

For many this comes as a great disappointment—McLuhan after all had insisted that "since TV, nobody is happy with mere book knowledge of French or English poetry. The unanimous cry now is 'Let's talk French,' or 'Let the Bard be heard.' " With no one really able to prove that even *Sesame Street* results in notable increases in ability, more and more TV reformers have settled for simply trying to get violence and gore off children's programming. This is difficult, because every cartoon made since 1945 still airs constantly. Still, many of the newly produced shows have eliminated the inventive, anarchic destruction of the old predator-prey shows. No more accordion-pleated burnt-to-a-cinder falling-two-thousand-feet-to-the-canyon-floor coyotes—now there are animated raccoons who say things like "It never hurts to be self-assertive," or space aliens named Derf who announce, "I'm scared to be around earthlings. Every day you fight and kill one another." One hopes the children don't notice that the gory cartoons of yore are carefully, patiently animated, while the modern versions, though their tone may be uplifting, are as crude and cheap as turn-of-the-century nickelodeons.

Since programming proves so stubbornly hard to upgrade, others put their hopes in the technology itself—as the machine improves, so will the experience. "Sometime in this decade the boob tube's going to get a silicon implant," writes Erik Davis in a *Village Voice* article about High Definition TV. "The principal effects will be an amping of *detail.* We'll not only data-binge on the range of channels but on the *depth* of those channels." And the TV will connect to more than the cable—"Tubing in the future will mean an endlessly hyphenated relationship with the shiny black pleasure machines. TV/VCR/CD/Laser Disc/PC . . . interfaces will get close and comfy because in order to get the most from our machines, our bodies and theirs have got to groove. . . . *Watching* becomes *using,* and hopefully *playing.*"

In the long run, the enthusiasts insist, this will lead to a McLuhan-Fuller sort of triumph that does business under the name "virtual reality." Before the decade is out, they say, we may be wearing bodysuits complete with earphones and glasses that will project images so that we become "literally immersed." Those "cyberspaces" may transform work life, as users "move down virtual hallways, entering the virtual offices of colleges, visiting virtual conference rooms and marketing centers where virtual products are displayed, pausing to read virtual bulletin boards, and so on." It may transform the bedroom—there is already a branch of the virtual reality industry called dildonics. According to reporter Douglas Martin, a seventy-year-old Timothy Leary came to New York recently for a $19-a-head lecture on his new enthusiasm, virtual reality. He said Huck Finn worked okay as a book but would be even better as a virtual reality video in which "viewers could twist the plot to suit their fancy." Some of this magic already exists. You don't have to wait to play virtual golf—there are already a hundred and fifty indoor courses around the country where you can challenge the famous courses by hitting the ball into a video screen. And all day long on television, a company was offering a set of videotapes that put you "in the cockpit" of modern airplanes so you could "spew death and destruction" or "rain terror." "You're in an A-10 Warthog, blasting twenty-one hundred shells a minute into enemy targets."

All this connectedness, the technologists assure us, will finally alter the way we use TV—will turn us from consumers into producers, or at least participants. "Instead of passively receiving information dished out by a handful of newspaper or TV stations, we'll select the news that interests us most via an interactive electronic journalism network," one partisan posits. "We'll receive detailed reporting in specific cases, and even choose how the information looks and sounds—the typefaces, which images are still and which move, whether to see pictures or hear a broadcast." Exit the couch potato, enter the sofa-bound Venus's-flytrap, reaching out hungrily for nourishing electronic morsels.

"Far out!" you're clearly supposed to say. "Where can I buy it?" But are such advances actually so profound? When you think about it, the new technology doesn't really seem very staggering. The revolution clearly came with the invention of television, when you could carry sight and sound from distant places into your home and do it abundantly and cheaply. The rest—the bodysuits and the laser discs and so on—are add-ons, refinements, and they do not fundamentally alter the limits of the technology. They are attempts to overcome through more technology the frustrations of living in an electronic world. They're like the gadget featured in a CNN report—a fake window being sold to hospitals as "the nucleus of stress reduction systems." The "window," backlit by 108 computer-operated lights, simulates the day from "sunrise to the orange glow of sunset," and was demonstrably worth twenty thousand dollars because patients placed next to it got better faster than if they were surrounded by four blank walls. "Windows represent light—light is the essence of life on this planet," said the inventor. But most of us, most of the time, can just open a real window. Or play real golf, or have real sex. We can't spew death and destruction from an A-10 Warthog, but perhaps that's just as well.

But it's not just real reality that electronics supplants; it's the other arts that try to mediate reality. Television and all its brother media boast constantly about their superiority. You're *there,* live! In fact, these machines are almost literally superficial—they are stuck with what things look like, with surfaces. Consider, just by contrast, the book, a form in disrepute with the up-to-date. "While a book requires special treatment and care and can only be fully explored after a long learning process," writes Edward Rothstein in *The New York Times,* "electronic devices are, despite adult fears, nearly indestructible and instantly accessible. The buttons allow free and fearless play." Personally, I've broken more electronic devices than I've broken books, but, that aside, compare the power of the two. An author, in a sentence or even half a sentence, can conjure up any locale from Paris to Pluto, can flip backward and forward in time, can take you inside the minds of her characters. She's in no measure bound by what she can take a picture of. TV can show you a face, saving you the work of imagining what that face would look like, but it can't get behind the face, or it can do so only clumsily, by having a character talk. Only the finest directors and actors overcome the technology's inherent obsession with surfaces. The *real* tight interface is between book and reader—the world of the book is plugged right into your brain, never mind the bodysuit.

In fact, the technology of TV is largely banal, dull, despite all the grandiose claims of its partisans. The *Times* recently reported on a study by two researchers at the Bank Street College of Education who watched four boys and five girls aged nine and ten as they played with a videodisc machine. "Within thirty minutes of experimentation, the children had learned not only to use the machine but how to play the disc in slow-motion, reverse, and fast-forward," the researchers reported in awestruck wonderment. "Some children made up games, freezing images or running them backwards. . . . Later, in class, children improvised silly dance steps to represent each of the different options, which one youngster would call out at random, shouting, for example, 'Fast Forward!' 'Slow,' 'Reverse,' 'Freeze.' For the children, the world of the player, far from being alien, was a world of play." Maybe so, but how many buttons are there on a laser disc player? And for how many hours is it fun to make a movie go on fast forward? Pretty soon, I would think, it's time for *Super Sloppy Double Dare.*

Even if electronics can't promise automatic enlightenment, though, can't we still hope for exceptional programs? Programs that will from time to time change the way we see the world, programs that will open our hearts and minds as much as the best books—and do it in a grand, mass, simultaneous way? We can hope, and sometimes we will be rewarded—*Twin Peaks* you can argue over, but Ken Burns's *Civil War* was a success. (It's curious, though, that what many called the best TV show ever relied so heavily on still photos, and on readings from letters, since these hardly take advantage of TV's supposed technical gifts. In some ways it was more like a wonderfully illustrated book that talented people read aloud.) And some of the nature shows, and *60 Minutes*, and *Frontline*, and so on. No doubt about it—there is good stuff on TV.

But even here there's a catch. Even magnificent programs, or the smaller good things that happen each day, are doomed, I think, not to make much difference. This is because of the characteristic that really sets TV apart—not its ability to transmit sight and sound, but its ubiquitousness. There it stands, twenty-four hours a day, ready to pour out information and amusement. Here, as a result, we sit, taking in that information and amusement for many hours a day—for most people, a fifth or more of their waking life. Certain people have spent as much as that time reading, I suppose, but not many—TV is the first mass ubiquitous medium. A day of watching TV, Raymond Williams once wrote, is like "having read two plays, three newspapers, and three or four magazines on the same day that one has been to a variety show and a lecture and a football match." In societies like Britain and the United States, he continued, "more drama is watched in a week or weekend, by the majority of viewers, than would have been watched in a year or in some cases a lifetime in any previous historical period."

Which means that if something exceptional happens it hardly matters—it is quickly forgotten, averaged out, eroded by this ceaseless flood. On *Good Morning America,* they're interviewing Teddy Kollek, the mayor of Jerusalem, who is saying a few interesting things about a recent visit from Václav Havel. But as soon as he's finished, or maybe slightly before, the host is saying, "Mr. Mayor—always outspoken, always feisty, always good to see you. How to prepare for a record invasion of gypsy moths that may be coming when *Good Morning America* continues." If the only TV you heard all day was this five-minute talk with Teddy Kollek, it might linger in your mind—you could mull it over. But it's instantly replaced by a man who's talking about egg masses and how a female gypsy moth resembles a 747, and then it's Omelette McMuffin and Tom Berenger and a chat with Brent Musburger and a movie review and a plug for tomorrow's program about Kent State and an extensive chat between the various hosts about their upcoming trip to the British Isles, all in less than an hour.

The problem is not that the individual segments are too short—you can say a lot in a few minutes. It's that each line of thought is instantly replaced by another. The Discovery Channel ran an excellent program called *The Primal Mind,* for instance, which discussed the philosophical difference between European churches with their heaven-pointed spires and the architecture of the Southwest

Indians, who built their dwellings so they would look like natural extensions of the hills. If it was the only show I'd seen all week, it might have made an impact. But very few people watch one hour a week. Most watch twenty-five or thirty-five hours, and the vast bulk of it is not exceptional—it's Carson and the news and MTV and the *NFL Today* and so on. You read one book at a time and it takes several days, so there's some chance of its sinking in. But mostly TV just flows along.

Expecting that one exceptional program will matter is like expecting that you can eat french fries and gravy all week and then lower your cholesterol with a single spear of broccoli on Sunday night. One jog a month doesn't do anything more than maybe remind you your muscles are weak. After the show about primitive people, the Discovery Channel ran documentaries on European marmots, Gold Cup hydroplane racing, and "Lobsters—Knights of the Sea." At 8:00 A.M. the Learning Channel informed viewers that Swedenborg invented an aeroplane in the seventeenth century. At 8:05 it discussed modems and at 8:30 gave a review for the college boards and at 9:00 taught you to hit a golf ball out of a sand trap ("Hit the sand somewhere behind the ball") and at 9:30 hectored you about your return of service, and at 10:00 sold you a grinder that makes bread crumbs in a baggie and at 10:30 reminded you that when you add the applejack brandy to your port sauce you should do it away from the flame, and at 11:30 took you to a numismatics convention ("One of your prettiest nudes or seminudes is a Goya-type woman standing at the edge of a note from the Corn Exchange Bank of DeSoto, Nebraska—I tell you, she's everybody's dream date"), and at noon cautioned you to cook crabs till they float, and at 1:00 assured you that butter is "easily recognized by the liver," and at 2:00 showed you an impressive machine that shakes almond trees so the nuts will fall down and Hershey's can pick them up. And so on all day and night.

No one watches it all, but virtually no one watches just one thing a day, much less a week or a month. If God decided to deliver the Ten Commandments on the *Today* show, it's true he'd have an enormous audience. But the minute he was finished, or maybe after he'd gotten through six or seven, it would be time for a commercial and then a discussion with a pet psychiatrist about how to introduce your dog to your new baby.

A few years ago an isolated Colombian Indian tribe, the Kogi, decided they needed to send a message to the rest of the world. The snowpack that watered their mountain range was disappearing; their seers insisted that human activity was destroying the environment around the planet. So they broke their strict prohibition against contact with the outside world and allowed a BBC producer into their villages to film a documentary. "It was not at all clear to them what 'the BBC' was," the producer said later. "Some clearly formed the view that it was a kin group of some sort." But though they had no idea that the world was round, they grasped the magical power of television. Their message—that they "have seen the changes start that mark the end of life; the world is beginning to die"—could be instantly and simultaneously transmitted to most of the people of the world. So the film crew came, with helicopters and lights and cameras; the documentary was made, and it was shown in Britain and America and around the world, and quite a few people watched, and many of them must have found it sobering, for here was a long-lived culture speaking out of nowhere at the same time and with the same message as our leading scientists. It was uncanny. But then it was over, and something else came on, and the warning passed unheeded. The only environmentalist who has really made effective use of television is Jacques Cousteau, and he proves the point. When you think of Cousteau you don't think of a particular program or a particular issue—just an endlessly repeated and demonstrated love for the ocean, millions of frames of the world beneath the waves.

Let us imagine we are, with Marshall McLuhan, living in a global, or even a national, village. Each evening we gather around the campfire to listen to stories. All the original "campfire cultures" understood the importance of repetition. They understood it out of necessity—since they couldn't write things down easily or at all, and since they certainly couldn't put them on tape for later retrieval, they had no choice but to repeat their essential messages and ideas over and over. These "primary oral" cultures may sound boring to us—the same stories again and again. But of course they weren't exactly the same. Told by different tellers they might sound different. A little added here, a little subtracted there. By such methods the great national epics were "written," codified in a million performances. Imagine their power (for good or for ill) to order lives! There were not a hundred channels—a hundred campfires in the village each with its own epic. There was one. No multiplex—a single theater, where the same movie, perhaps in installments, showed year after year. This kind of culture no longer exists, except in isolated instances like the Kogi, and not just because we've invented writing. It can't exist because there's no longer any way to agree on what's essential. Once, survival depended on both the transmission of certain information (say, how to hunt so there'd be animals left for next year) and on the creation of a cohesive community. Though that may still be true, we don't perceive it to be so.

Still, as McLuhan realized, there's a lot of the tribal villager left in us. We respond to repetition, and TV offers it. It shows a million different programs, but they're not *that* different. Where English teachers once identified the six conflicts in literature (man against man, man against nature, and so on) they could now list for their students the six sitcom plots: man struck on head gets amnesia, woman has half of a winning lottery ticket, man dislikes his daughter's boyfriend, man finds himself in an unconventional living arrangement (for instance, his roommates are three busty cheerleaders). HA!, a "comedy" channel, just by coincidence showed five sitcoms in one day that turned on the theme of a wife's jealousy of her husband's pretty new secretary. Murder is the most common device of all, of course—instead of happening nearby once or twice in a lifetime, it happens many times a day. And certain unimpeachable moral themes repeat as well: five or six years of watching *M*A*S*H* leaves a residue of certain liberal values—an appreciation of diversity, say, and an affection for mild rebelliousness. The most powerful repeating element is obviously the commercial. Advertisers, the most diligent students of human nature, know that it is useless to advertise just once or twice—the ad must be repeated a hundred times, a thousand times, till it "penetrates" the "clutter." Particular advertisements ("Coke is it") and the conceits of ads in general—that physical labor is a painful ordeal, that you are ugly and small and secreting offensive flakes and fluids—come to order our idea of the world because they appear before us so constantly.

Against this tide, the exceptional drowns. By its very name the exceptional is an exception, and since the rules are repeated so often (tribal villagers would have starved if they had spent as much time around their campfires as we do around ours), it can make little headway. I recently came across a yellowing UNESCO report on television, issued in 1953, when most of its member countries were just beginning to acquire the technology. There was apparently a hot debate under way over how long each day the TV station (in most nations one, perhaps two or three, certainly not a hundred) should operate. "Television constitutes an enormous drain on creative talent," it reported. "It is difficult if not impossible to provide every day of the week good dramatic shows, good entertainment, good educational broadcasting, and good children's programmes. The result of long hours of programmes is bound to be that quality becomes the exception." I think, thirty-seven years later, they have been proven right, and another thirty-seven will only prove them righter still. At our campfire we will find little to help us order our lives intelligently. When we do happen across such things, they will be swamped by the endless multiplying programs and guests and topics and facts. (The single most important skill for any talk show host is the ability to cut off her guests tactfully so she can get on to the next item.) We cling therefore, to the repeating elements—they may not be nourishing, but at least they are familiar. And as every great teacher of every great faith has told us, what we do and see each day is what shapes us, not how we behave or pretend to behave on special occasions.

Sometime After Midnight

Nights are as different, one from another, as days. Tonight, to the southwest, banks of clouds close in one corner of the sky—instead of seeing, as the cosmologists insist, toward the start of time and the edge of the universe, you could see just a rounded edge of black. But the rest of the sky was lit up—moon enough to run a trail of rippling white across the pond, and when it set the million stars were joined by a billion others. Even then sight didn't altogether fail me: on all but the inkiest nights you can feel your way through the darkness, picking out patterns like the gaps in trees that demarcate trails. And the noise—we think of the woodland creatures bedding down for the night, but of course many of them are just rising. Several coyote howled somewhere far in the distance; a mouse rustled across the nylon on the tent flap; on the pond a fish jumped now and again, slipping back into the water with a liquid *plonk* that died as soon as it had sounded. And a mosquito sawed in my ear, of course.

We've all but lost the night—twelve hours in twenty-four the information the planet provides goes unseen, not because it's dark but because it's light. McLuhan referred to electric light as "pure information, without any content to restrict its transforming and informing power." But you could argue as easily that each night at sundown we are hooded—a blanket of light cast over our heads that keeps us from seeing out into the dark. It doesn't take much light to obscure the night sky—a streetlight or two in the immediate vicinity, a city of any size over the hill. "All urban nights are the same," says Kohak. Even if you can look up through the tangle of buildings, you can't see the stars—maybe, sometimes, a planet is visible. And the moon—but never, ever, the moonlight, the way it washes the ground or on a foggy night fills the air with diffuse paleness. And most nights of our lives we don't even look—we just eliminate the dark, with our lights and with the television set, which connects us to an endless brightly colored never-flagging day.

It rarely occurs to us how much intelligence about the world a light erases. We link darkness with ignorance—the Dark Ages. But wisdom gathers after nightfall too. For millennia the starry skies were revered as the source of much wisdom—the sciences got their start tracking the constellations. Astrology has fallen on hard times. (There were two mentions of it on TV this day. One was a sermon by a Reverend Kennedy of a TV church in Coral Ridge, Florida, who argued that all the signs of the zodiac foretold Christ's coming. The other was on an NBC program called *House Party,* where an astrologer who'd cast a royal horoscope said it was highly possible that Di was playing around, and that Fergie's daughters will be feisty and difficult, particularly Eugenie, who is, after all, an Aries.) But if we don't need astrology anymore, we still need the night sky.

During the day, when the sun blots out the stars and confines our sight to distances of a few miles, it's no wonder that we consider ourselves and our concerns all-important. Even the sun, the one distant object that we can see, seems to have a direct one-to-one relationship with our planet, to be there for our use. But at night this illusion ends—suddenly we can see the infinite around us. It is impossible to stand under the stars and not feel small. The ancients erred in thinking earth stood at the center of things. But we err, far more grievously, when, night after night, despite all our telescopes and spacecraft, we forget that anything else even exists. Nighttime has always inspired awe, an awe TV sometimes tries to borrow. "There's something about the power of the moon," coos a blonde in a perfume commercial. "I feel its power instinctively. Possess the power—Luna Mystique." But you can't possess it, of course—you can only gaze upon it, or switch on the flickering haha of prime time, our new name for night.

4:00 A.M.

It's time for *Financial Freedom and Wealth Building in America Today*, a program that comes to you from the beautiful Outrigger Waikiki on the sand in Honolulu. John Davidson is the host—in recent years the star of *Hollywood Squares.* I first remember him from an ancient sitcom in which Sally Field played his wife and she could read his mind. Anyway, he appears impervious to age, and he's here to introduce you to David Del Dotto, a "self-made millionaire," a veteran of "countless television appearances," a "frequent visitor to congressional offices," "America's best-known success merchant," and a man who would like you to send him $367 in exchange for some books he's written on how you can buy foreclosed real estate. He gives good spiel, especially the story about the guy who sold so much foreclosed real estate that he was able to bring his mother over from Bulgaria for a visit, but I was more intrigued with the unlikely "celebrities" who kept appearing to endorse his approach—Miss Hawaii, for instance, who urged "you youngsters and college people" to buy the books.

The idea of standing under the stars and feeling how small you are—that's not a television idea. Everything on television tells you the opposite—that you're the most important person, and that people are all that matter. "We do it all for you"; "Have it your way"; the immortal "This Bud's for you." The endless parade of jesters to entertain *you*, the obsequious newscasts that bring the story *you* want to see right to *your* living room. It's what *you* want—"The consumer is our God," the chairman of MTV Networks told *Rolling Stone.* The man in charge of scheduling videos added, "Millions of dollars are spent to find out what the viewers want to see." "We need some more people sucking up to us because we're going to be spending obscene amounts of money."

This ceaseless toadying and curtseying and currying of our favor—for we, after all, can provide the dollars and the ratings they desire—inevitably distort our view of the world. What counts? People count. If Brandon Tartikoff, the former NBC programming genius, rewrote the book of Genesis, people would be created on Day One and Noah's Ark would be filled with zany folks—not much room for animals, especially the boring ones. The stars in the night sky hold no interest to advertisers, for they don't reflect us. The stars that *do* reflect us are the kind that appear on talk shows. Since we can't all appear on TV, our race needs some representatives, and these are the people filling the couch next to Regis and Kathie Lee. If they were of interest because they were actors, Johnny would ask them questions about acting—"How did you conjure up the mood for that scene?" Instead, we want to know about their lives, and the lives of other stars they have "worked with." They are of interest because they are other people, and that they are usually normal to the point of boredom only adds to their appeal because they are stand-ins for us. By the very act of being important, they redeem the lifetime we spend watching them. Most cultures, historically, have put something else—God or nature or some combination—at the center. But we've put them at the periphery. A consumer society doesn't need them to function, and it can't tolerate the limits they might impose; there's only need for people.

Television's unique contribution to this process is the creation of celebrities who are celebrated almost entirely for being celebrities—they're "legends" because TV has so much time to fill. Here's Robert Morley in a studio kitchen cooking with "celebrity" guest Jo Anne Worley, late of *Laugh-In.* Did someone say *Laugh-In?* Here's Arte Johnson, the man who used to say "Very interesting but stupid," a line my little brother repeated about four hundred times a day for several months in 1971. Johnson is hosting a celebrity putting contest to benefit the Hugh O'Brian Youth Foundation. Jack Carter is putting—"This is the most fun you can have with your clothes on," he says in his waggish way. Here's Zsa Zsa Gabor's *daughter* on *Inside Report.* She's making her living as a stand-up comic—her ghostwriter is Mickey Rooney, Jr. She's telling stories about Christmas with her pop, Conrad Hilton.

It's almost impossibly sad to watch these fading celebrities sometimes. We're stuck with having to figure out what it means that Gilligan—Bob Denver, who can be seen in almost every home in America every day—is twenty-five years older than his castaway self and here he is explaining to Sig, on *Sig's Celebrity Kitchen,* about how he works at boat shows. They build him an island, and he sits on the island and signs autographs. "I've got them from thirty-five all the way down that grew up with me," he says—this man was also Maynard G. Krebs, of course. He's cooking "noodle, bean, and beef casserole," and talking about his friend the Skipper, who died recently. "I did a lot of personal appearances with him the last twenty years. We got rescued wherever there was a body of water." It's nearly impossible to be more well-known than Gilligan—what tiny percentage of Americans, shown a picture of him in his bosun's cap, couldn't identify him? And yet—scary thought—he seems pathetic now. Passed by, the way we will all be passed by in time. It's different, a little, if you're famous for something great like writing a symphony—maybe for a hundred years, or five hundred, you'll be recalled. But in the fullness of time it doesn't really matter—the densest pupil of the most minor Greek philosopher could have told you that, or the least earnest Buddhist, or the most hedonistic Navajo, or the most illiterate early Christian. We, however, are too busy watching *Rodeo*

Drive, the gossip game show where "the glitter meets the dirt," which begins with "seven concealed words" connected with John Goodman, Mr. T, and Raisa Gorbachev. "Janet Jackson or Jesse Jackson—who's had a marriage annulled?" "Fact or rumor—Whoopi Goldberg is an honorary member of the Harlem Globetrotters." (Fact—also Geraldo Rivera is an attorney.)

Human beings—any one of us, and our species as a whole—are not all-important, not at the center of the world. That is the one essential piece of information, the one great secret, offered by any encounter with the woods or the mountains or the ocean or any wilderness or chunk of nature or patch of night sky. I can sit on the knob above the pond and see the hills stretch off into the blue-gray distance; I can hide myself quietly on the edge of a glade and watch the deer and the chipmunks and the bugs and the flowers and the old tree rotting; I can lie on my back and watch the vultures circle—and I would be a fool to think this had anything to do with me. To think that it wasn't here before me, or that it didn't exist for its own reasons, quite independent of my need for beauty or "solitude." It's true that if I wanted to I could destroy it—set fire to it, or develop it for a ski resort. And we as a species have the power, by forever putting ourselves first, to end it forever with our weapons, or damage it terribly by changing the climate or eroding the ozone or altering the other fundamental systems on which it depends. We have the *power* to make the world fit our "anthropocentric" or people-centered vision. But that obviously doesn't mean, wouldn't mean, that this view of the world was correct. Some environmentalists have begun to talk about "deep ecology" in recent years—about the idea that we must see the earth as a whole, and that if we insist on dominating everything, we'll create for ourselves an unlivable world and so on and so forth. But this vital information comes best from the encounter with the real world—the *real* real world, the one that was here before us.

And yet it is so hard to remember. A man named Edward Abbey wrote a book called *Desert Solitaire* about twenty years ago, a book that will be remembered and read in the same way *Walden* is remembered and read. It's the story of a winter he spent as the ranger at Arches National Monument outside Moab, Utah, and near the beginning he writes, "I am here . . . to confront, immediately and directly if it's possible, the bare bones of existence, the elemental and fundamental, the bedrock which sustains us. I want to be able to look at and into a juniper tree, a piece of quartz, a vulture, a spider, and see it as it is in itself, devoid of all humanly ascribed qualities." Since he wrote that, they've put a paved road through Arches, and an endless line of Winnebagos crawls along it. Sometimes a hundred people stand under Delicate Arch—the first time I went there I ran into an old college friend, and so instead of the bedrock that sustains us I filled my mind with reports on classmates. The local news on the CBS affiliate had a special travel report on the Moab area—"Most of the roads are well paved . . . with plenty of spots to pull over and enjoy a view," the jovial host said. "For the more adventurous, fifty-five dollars will buy you a day of four-wheeling in the backcountry. You'll splash through creek beds, between narrow rock walls." And over and over again on MTV there was a Jon Bon Jovi video set on the hills above Moab. They constructed a falling-down drive-in movie theater for the video, which is not about the juniper or the quartz or the vulture. It's about Mr. Bon Jovi, a "six-gun lover" who's dying, in the words of the title, in a *Blaze of Glory*.

In the world where we live most of the time, we are constantly in contact with the artifacts of man. I wake up in a room, I shower in a tub, I climb into a car and drive down a street lined with buildings, listening to people joke on the radio. Human society is where we're destined to spend most of our lives. The distinctive company of our own species is right for us, and sweet—the last thing we need is a nation of backpacking hermits. Human beings count, as individuals and en masse. We have duties owed each other and owed ourselves. But when there's little or no regular contact with the natural world, with the *wildness* found even in five-acre woodlots or on deserted waterfronts, then we start to feel that human society is all there is. "The consumer society," writes Kohak, "is here realizing the nightmarish vision of Karl Marx, for whom the human is the being who confronts the world and encounters in it only the product of his own labor." The consumer society, exemplified by television, is obsequious in its attentions, and promises you all happiness. Whereas the mountain is indifferent. It promotes a brand of existentialism—it's hard, sitting on a mountain, to think that there's some great and exalted and sensible reason for your presence on this planet. But it's a joyful existentialism, because we so clearly can fit in—because the world in which we're inexplicably thrown is magnificent, sweet. It's within our power, too, to leave much of it alone. To witness its rightness. That may be our real importance—as the only creatures who can fully comprehend how correct and harmonious the world is. Scientists have a stronger sense of this than most of us, and that is because they spend more time with wildness—not in the woods, necessarily, but through a microscope or a telescope. They know, many of them, that mere appreciation, the attempt to understand marvels for their own sake, is worth a life's work.

All this seems perfectly obvious sitting alone on a mountain, and a little overgrand sitting at my desk. The trick is to find practical, human ways to show that we understand we're not at the center of the universe. In some cases this means limiting ourselves, individually and as societies—taking as little water and land as we can, putting as little junk into the air as we can manage, working to protect the biological diversity of the planet not because it may someday yield a cure for cancer but just because it is. In other cases it means celebrating the wild world that's around us everywhere. *Everywhere.* In New York City in the spring the great eastern bird migration turns Prospect Park and Central Park into twittering convention centers filled with an immense variety of birds. A few weeks later, along the beaches of Brooklyn and Queens, the horseshoe crabs, oldest unchanged living creatures (so old they have *copper-*based blood), come onshore in great waves to mate. In any other time and place, these would be occasions for great civic festivals, and they should be now.

Like a week alone in the woods, these annual migrations reinforce an old and dying message, a message that environmentalists need to hear as strongly as anyone. It's true we live in "an environment," and that's important—we need clean air to breathe and clean water to drink. But "an environment" is a human affair; its successes and failures are judged in human terms. It should have a boundary to it, an ending. We live on a *planet,* too, which we share with innumerable forms of life. It is a buzzing, weird, stoic, abundant, glorious planet—all of it matters and all of it is glorious.

5:00 A.M.

For the two or three hundredth time today, a worried, expensively casual man with incipient hair loss is trying to place a phone call. He is phoning Phoenix, but somehow manages to dial Fiji instead, where his call is answered by a partying native on a beach. This mix-up is odd—it seems to imply that if you misdial you are likely to reach a location phonetically similar to your intended destination—e.g., Peking, not Peoria. In fact, the area code for Phoenix is 602, while to reach Fiji you must call 011-679. But never mind—that's not the man's problem. His problem is that he has switched phone companies and his new carrier won't give him "immediate credit for wrong numbers." It's unclear why he can't wait a few days for his mistake to be righted—by all appearances he has more money than he knows what to do with—but he goes into a petulant sulk, whining to the operator that this never happened with AT&T. (Apparently he's spent much of his life misdialing.) The operator says, understandably, "You're not dealing with AT&T." "I am now," he says, slamming down the receiver as his disgusted look gives way to a smile of rueful triumph.

AT&T ads, as Michael Arlen documented in his book *Thirty Seconds,* are more carefully produced than most feature films. When you're selling something as intangible as the phone connection to someone's house, you need to rally primal emotion. For years they relied on sentiment—"Reach out and touch." But in the years since the courts ended AT&T's monopoly, they've had to raise even stronger feelings, like fear of humiliation. Their main campaign, to persuade customers not to heed the blandishments of MCI or Sprint and switch their service, has featured a parade of harassed yuppies, all of whom have made the mistake of going over to the other side. "What is *with* these people?" fumes one woman as she sits in her airy, enormous studio—she does some kind of work that involves looking at slides on a light table. "A month ago they called me—'Save big over AT&T.' So I switched. Bill came. Big savings didn't. It turned out they'd compared their special discount plan to AT&T's regular prices." She has an indignant catch in her voice—a "Get a load of this" tone, as if she's caught diet guru Richard Simmons eating sticks of butter. "*Now* they tell me? C'mon, guys. If this is all I get I'm not hanging around." The booming male voice of AT&T fills the air: "People who thought they could do better than AT&T are coming back for the real value. Aren't you glad you never left?" We cut back to the woman, sitting on her couch, smiling and shaking her head, sadder but wiser. "Unreal," she says.

Then there's the overweight, balding black man. He double-parks his car on a city street, and jumps out in the rain to make a call from a pay phone, the picture of aggressive self-confidence. "Huh, huh," he chuckles. "This is going to be a piece of cake, right—pull over and make a fast call. But I'm using this other long-distance company." By now the rain is falling harder—it's one of those open-air booths, so most of him is sticking out into the downpour. "Now, first they have me dial all these numbers just to get them. Then I get to dial the number I'm calling. Then I have to dial all these other numbers." As the black man urgently pecks with his big fingers at the little keys, a cop arrives to ticket his car. The caller doesn't notice until it's too late—then he dashes futilely out into the street, arms akimbo, raincoat flapping pathetically, as the cop drives away. "So yeah—huh, huh, huh—I made the call. To the tune of thirty-five dollars. Huh, huh, huh." The joke's on him, just as it was on the man calling Fiji and the lady with no big savings, and all the other characters in this memorable series. They had been taken in, suckered by the sweet talk of a better life with MCI. They had suffered humiliation, not because they had gotten a parking ticket or Fiji on the phone, but because they had not been tough, gritty—they had listened to the siren song of change, and parted with long-established habit. (No consumer habit, except maybe Coke, is as old as AT&T.) Now the sirens they were hearing belonged to the police. They had been fools, but at least they had learned a lesson: Stay with what you know. Don't risk disappointment. Better to keep your old bill than find your new one is no lower. Better to stay on the right side of the cops. Not nice to fool Mother Bell. "Aren't you glad you never left?"

I've tried, in the preceding pages, to describe some of the information that the modern world—the TV world—is missing. Information about the physical limits of a finite world. About sufficiency and need, about proper scale and real time, about the sensual pleasure of exertion and exposure to the elements, about the human need for community and for solid, real skills. About the good life as it appears on TV, and about other, perhaps better, lives. As I said at the outset, human desires count. I think the signals the natural world sends us—the seven warmest years on record all occurring in the last decade, for instance—are signals that our desires need to change.

Even if everyone agreed, this would be an outlandishly difficult task. Switching from our present headlong trajectory toward personal lives and societies and economies that instead stress frugality and sustainability would demand enormous ingenuity. Even among those who are convinced such a life would be richer, change is hard—I still live in a fashion as close to my suburban upbringing as to my ideal of engagement. In part this is due to the difficulty of trying to live against the majority—you can vow to give up your car and ride the bus, but if your area has failed to provide decent and regular public transportation your vow will soon fade. In part, it's probably due to ingrained flaws in our nature—greed, or desire for status, or for power—which should never be ignored or wished away, and which have troubled people in all times and all ages. But in part, too, it's due to a very particular feature of the modern world, especially the television world.

The AT&T ads exemplify the conservatism of an advanced consumer society. One of the functions of advertising, and more broadly of television as a whole, is to reinforce the way we're used to doing things, and one of its most potent tools is ridicule. These saps have changed their *long-distance company* and been humiliated—what if they had decided to change, say, their expensive taste in cars and clothes? What if they decided to change their jobs, alter their life-styles? The consumer society can adapt to change—indeed, in the name of growth it must sometimes encourage it—but the form of adaptation is usually akin to what a marketer would call "brand management." That is, confronted with the rise of people interested in good nutrition, no advertiser worth his reduced sodium content would encourage people simply to eat less packaged food or dine lower on the food chain. Instead, they "extend" their brand by creating slightly different products that perhaps can be marketed at higher margins—breakfast cereals, say, studded with slivers of almond because people believe that "nutty goodness" will help lower their cholesterol. Or they reposition their brand slightly. If you had recently begun watching McDonald's ads, for instance, you would likely think it was an enormous recycling company that happened to sell hamburgers on the side. During the buildup to the Iran-Iraq war, Cadillac, whose cars barely averaged sixteen miles to the gallon in city driving, added the tag line "as responsible to own as they are responsive to drive" to some of their commercials, in order to "reassure prospective buyers that they would not be out of step with the times by purchasing a Cadillac."

Or consider Cheerios, which built a successful franchise based on the essential tastelessness of their cereal. Combined with its mildly humorous shape, this made it a perfect food for young children. Its advertising agency, however, had clearly decided to cash in on the popular adult belief that oats were a magic bullet against heart disease. Two men, obviously busy executives, sit in a dining room sharing a power breakfast. One of them—the younger, flightier one—complains about how difficult it is to "know what to believe" about nutrition, what with all the conflicting claims and so on. He fears, obviously, the humiliation of making the wrong choice—of choosing the MCI of breakfast cereals or, worse yet, some nonbrand, some bowl of berries or brown rice. The older fellow, his mentor, takes a second to set him straight. Cheerios, he says, is nutrition made simple, because "you don't need any more problems." Change has been successfully contained, if not to Cheerios proper then to its new companion, Honey Nut Cheerios. This ad is instructive—all sorts of people are confusing you with their ideas about how you should act in the world. But there's no need to be confused—stick with the old, the tried-and-true. On TV, of course, the old, the tried-and-true, means the artifacts of the consumer society, not whatever came before. They can change slightly, but not radically.

Allied with this fear of humiliation is television's carefully cultivated sense of hip, its ironic stance. Mark Crispin Miller wrote a brilliant essay in the 1980s that he titled "The Hipness Unto Death," pointing out that a great deal of the time when we are watching TV we know that it is stupid. That in fact we watch it because we know it is stupid and enjoy the feeling of superiority—of hipness—it provides. That is, TV more or less takes us into its confidence—it says, "You know it's silly to be watching Donna Reed reruns after thirty-five years, and we know it's silly. That's why we're packaging them in this funny way, with lots of jokes about how silly she is living in her 'dream house' and so on." What it doesn't say is, once you're swelled with this agreeable sense of of your hip superiority, you can be sold products as easily as a tribesman just emerging from the bush. Miller goes on to successfully deconstruct any number of shows and commercials (his *Family Feud* autopsy is a gem), but even he, I think, would have a hard time believing just how obvious TV has become in the last two or three years as it plays to our sense of hipness.

Take MTV as an example. The people who run the network face a potentially serious problem—their target audience is at the age when they might be attracted to "subversive" and uncontained ideas. And rock 'n' roll, defanged as it now is, still, by sheer volume if nothing else, raises the possibility of mild rebellion against the model consumer life-style. MTV's response has included a series of ads like this one:

> People who make TV
> COMMERCIALS
> use words just like these to
> COMMUNICATE A MESSAGE
> This practice is supposed to be
> SIMPLE AND EFFECTIVE
> These words . . . will hang out for 15 seconds
> until it's time
> for another
> COMMERCIAL
> These are words that could be saying something
> but they're not
> They're just sitting here
> LIKE YOU
> MTV

This ad is not designed, obviously, to make you stand up and turn off the TV and do something else. (MTV above all others requires lethargic torpor from its viewers.) It is designed to make you say, "Yeah, I'm hip. I'm just sitting here, but I'm under no illusion that I'm not—I'm not pretending to be doing something deep. I'm a couch potato." Others were following this lead—the brand-new HA! comedy network, appealing to an MTVish demographic, was constantly airing promos for itself with slogans like "I've got better things to do," a wink that makes it okay to sit and watch, say, twenty-four solid hours of Marlo Thomas reruns ("Gobs and Gobs of *That Girl*"). In the end, though,

MTV retained the title for most cynical commercial, a sixty-second spot that I saw during *Yo, MTV Raps.* Jonathan Demme, the certifiably hip filmmaker, was shown in close-up, just talking: "With MTV, obviously, the prime purpose of MTV is to entertain, and that's fine, but I think it would be terrific to see MTV try to become more a force for—in a small way, without intruding on their need to entertain—become some kind of force for social change and have kind of—to use MTV as some kind of consciousness-raising medium as well as an entertainment medium." Now, MTV doesn't want to raise our consciousness—if it did, it wouldn't show so much Lycra. If it did, it would just go out and try, not show Jonathan Demme talking about how it would be nice if it did. But MTV knows that at this particular moment there are lots of kids thinking about social change, or thinking that they should be thinking about social change—about the environment, say. So it allows—encourages—them to pretend that they are so hip that it's happening almost by osmosis, simply by looking at Jonathan Demme.

TV retains its power in part because it's trained us not to take it seriously. This emperor is so confident that he announces constantly that he has no clothes—he makes jokes about it. "See—no pants, hahahaha. Back after this short commercial break." Watch David Letterman for a night to see what I mean. You can hardly deconstruct it—it's deconstructing itself. There's nothing on TV to push *against*; even if you're inclined to push, after a while you stop and are carried along for the ride. On a medium that mocks itself, seriousness does not play. If someone came on MTV, or any other spot on the dial, and began to say, "Hey, we should learn to walk instead of drive cars everywhere," GM would have nothing to fear. Trained to laugh, trained as ironists, trained to avoid anything that might make us foolish, we're all but inoculated against such messages. "Sounds like the Waltons." "Good night Johnboy." "Good night Grandma." TV has prepared us to defuse most bombs. When the twelve-year-olds on the new Mickey Mouse Club perform a long sketch spoofing the Home Shopping network ("If you were to buy the planet Saturn in any store, you might expect to pay twenty-five squajillion dollars"), they are not attacking the Home Shopping network. They are unconsciously ensuring that kids will watch it immune to its crudeness. Because they already know—they're in on the joke. If you think Home Shopping network's a tacky rip-off, you're a dweeb, because everyone already knows it's a tacky rip-off.

Television, writes Miller, "has us automatically deplore or ridicule all anger, fear, political commitment, deep belief, keen pleasure, exalted self-esteem, tremendous love; and yet while making all these passions seem unnatural, the medium persistently dwells on their darkest consequences, teasing the housebound spectator with hints of that intensity it has helped to kill." TV is sometimes accused of encouraging fantasies. Its real problem, though, is that it encourages—enforces, almost—a brute realism. It is anti-utopian in the extreme. We're discouraged from thinking that, except for a few new products, there might be a better way of doing things. I've discussed, for instance, the possibility that smaller, tighter, more self-sufficient communities might help us through our human and environmental problems. On TV, such communities, when portrayed at all, are invariably pictured as fanatic. Today's *Twilight Zone* repeat follows a motorist whose car breaks down—he spends the night in an inbred country town. "We've lived here for generations, independent of the outside world," they tell him. But instead of decent Amish, they are nutball maniacs who believe that the lighthouse on the coast is instructing them to kill the stranger. TV employs a consistent and mocking reductio ad absurdum with anything the slightest bit off center. Ever occur to you to give up TV for a while? A sitcom called *Mr. Belvedere* explores this subject—the main character is a butler, and in today's episode his family has sworn off the tube. As a result they become absurd. They play Simon Says. They dress up in hillbilly outfits and start a jug band. Without TV you'd be playing a kazoo. Think maybe you might give your family more time and attention instead of buying them stuff? Then watch the single cruelest ad on television. One after another, nice-looking old ladies appear on the screen to say what they want for Mother's Day. "You just give me your love and respect," says one. But underneath her chin, Joe Isuzu–fashion, appear the words "I'd like that nice desk organizer." Thanks, Hallmark, we really needed that.

That reduction to absurdity—that mocking, knowing snicker—is so sad, because it shuts people's ears to the promise of this particular moment. Which is, simply, this:

having immense amounts of technology available to us, this society could pick and choose those things that would create a life both sustainable and rich.

When you mention that in some ways people lived better a hundred years ago, the nearly automatic response is that they died at fifty. True enough—and I've never heard anyone seriously suggest giving up antibiotics and anesthesia and clean water. But perhaps we could, if we listened more carefully to the information of the natural world, come to terms with dying and spare ourselves the last anguished months hooked to machines. Almost no one suggests *abolishing* electricity—but a nation where nightfall meant a bulb or two and the elegance of candles, that's not so obviously ludicrous. We light candles for *romance,* for special occasions. Perhaps lighting them two or three times a week instead of turning on lamps and televisions would greatly increase the percentage of our lives that are romantic and special. Certainly it would let us see the sunset and the dark more easily; certainly it would cut down the light bill. Those of us who live in the north know that every few years a big snowstorm immobilizes us and turns off the power—and turns the world spectacularly peaceful. We forget that we have the power, and the right, to simulate the effects of a snowstorm as often as we want to.

We've now, as a species, lived through extremes. We know that people will flee from backbreaking labor at the first chance. But we might be starting to sense that the total abandonment of skilled and careful labor, the utter emancipation offered by light bulbs and machines, can be just as alienating, quite aside from their environmental dangers. And perhaps we're starting to sense something deeply human in a life less engaged with the world of consumption and growth and comfort offered by television, and more engaged with the world of balance and pleasure and elegant simplicity suggested by the natural world. You don't need to live in the country to understand these kinds of changes. City dwellers and suburbanites can continue to drive everywhere, hoping that the ever-progressing society will deliver hydrogen cars or solar cars or whatever other kinds of cars soon enough to save the atmosphere. Or they can begin to use existing technology—the bicycle, for instance. It's every bit as technological as an electric car, and as a significant minority of people have discovered, it's endlessly more elegant. On a bicycle you see the world around you—you notice hills that a car obliterates; you see neighborhoods at a pace that makes them real, not a blur. You save gas, of course, but you also hear your body again. TV can't appreciate this kind of elegance—on TV, you'd buy an Infiniti and drive it quickly to Jack LaLanne, where you can pay someone to let you sit on a stationary bicycle and pump away.

All the information offered by the natural world suggests that somewhere between the meaninglessness of lives lived in destitute struggle and the emptiness of life lived in swaddled affluence there is daily, ordinary life filled with meaning. Kohak, who lives in a small cabin in rural New Hampshire, writes: "A life wholly absorbed in need and its satisfaction, be it on the level of conspicuous consumption or of marginal survival, falls short of realizing the innermost human possibility of cherishing beauty, knowing the truth, doing the good, worshipping the holy." Life needn't be nasty, brutish, and short—we have the scientists and the engineers to thank for that. But it needn't, the clamor of TV notwithstanding, be infinite or utterly easy either. We don't need to go back to the Dark Ages—but how much further forward do we need to go? An efficient solar cell, yes. But what is there that we can't do now that we will be able to do when we've developed artificial intelligence and virtual reality and smart houses and all the other shiny promises of the technological future? What convenience or comfort does the average American life lack? If you could pick three conditions on earth to change in the next fifty years, would you want "advances"—Picturephones, virtual reality, computer shopping—or would you want more quiet, more community, cleaner air?

Sometimes TV offers what might be fables if they weren't facts. On C-SPAN this day, Congressman Gerry Sikorski, a Minnesota congressman, took to the rostrum of the House to raise the issue of children who are squished by automatic garage-door openers. "With fifty-five dead kids, we can't just shrug our shoulders," he said. Accidents are "turning that friendly open garage door of home into a fearsome death trap." That's obviously insufficient carnage to get us thinking about reducing our use of cars, and garages we can't do without—where would we put our stuff? But it never even occurs to Sikorski that we might at least eliminate automatic garage-door openers. They've somehow become vital to America—"that friendly open garage door of home." Instead, he demands passage of the

Automatic Garage Door Opener Safety Act to make sure that new automatic garage-door openers have reverse mechanisms.

Increasingly we live in a world filled with the equivalents of deadly garage-door openers, unnecessary items that offer us mild and insipid comfort at the price of a dangerous and uncomfortable planet, and at the price of any real relationship to the physical world. If you live in a suburban home and commute to a parking garage somewhere, that ten seconds opening the garage door might be nearly the only rain you ever feel.

Having been given the gift of light, can we use it to light our way on a dark night when we need to go somewhere—or must we keep using it as a floodlight, to wash out the darkness always and everywhere? Unlike all the other animals, who have these decisions made for them, we have to choose.

And we live at the curious moment when this choice matters—when aesthetic notions about the good life and community and sufficiency and so on, long the province of moral philosophers and preachers, coincide with interests of atmospheric chemists. You can look at our environmental problems like this—almost everyone on the planet is causing friction, some because they have too much and consume it wastefully, some because they have too little and must abuse the earth. Some drive Oldsmobiles and some chop down rain forests, but the life of each harms the planet, perhaps irreparably. Somewhere there is a mean. On the mountaintop you see it constantly in action—see life in balance, rolling on imperturbably, not growing, not shrinking. Over geological time it may change violently—these mountains were once volcanoes. But we don't live in geological time. This is the information nature whispers to us in biological time, in our time—it's the information drowned out by the familiar mocking laughter of TV. We can't go *live* in the woods by a lake—but we can go there long enough to listen, to hear. And come back not chastened but uplifted. So that we bike to work not because we have to but because it's the richest alternative. So that we live with less not because an economy in recession forces us to compromise but out of a distaste for the insulation from the real that "too much" ensures. That we grow some of our food not because we couldn't buy it but for the meeting with nature it affords and the sweetness of corn fresh picked. The question is not "Did the Indians have it right?" The question is not "Did the Amish have it right?" The question is "Can we, blessed with technology but also with nature, *get it right*?"

This sounds quaint to me, too, and improbable. How could it not? I grew up rapt with attention at the words and images on the screen. Darren and Gilligan and Mrs. Brady and Peter Jennings and all the rest—this was the real world. I assumed unconsciously that the information that poured from the TV into my quite similar suburban world was all the information there was, except for stuff about sex, which back then they couldn't show. But there's another real world. A realer world, maybe—certainly an older one. This world is full of information, information that grows inevitably in you the more time you spend there, the stiller you are. It is accessible to anyone anytime—to people in New York City who'll take the subway to the deserted beach; to people in Westchester who will ride a bike instead of drive a car, who will seek out the woods and hang the bird feeders and row the marshes along the Hudson. It's available, at least for a little while longer, to every one of us—especially to the comfortable in our society who most need to see it, hear it, feel it, *get it.* That's the one great hopeful possibility; this other world broadcasts round the clock, and in stereo and sensurround and smellavision. Its signal grows steadily fainter, and the noise of the modern world makes it ever harder to hear. But it's still there.

6:00 A.M.

You have smelly shoes over your eyes. Do you know who else is wearing eyeglasses? A dog is! And the dog is driving a car!" That's Harry Lorayne, who's selling his memory technique on WOR—he has remembered the names of all hundred people in the audience. On *The Flintstones,* Betty and Wilma are earning extra money by renting rooms to a pair of goateed jazz musicians who keep saying things like "way out groovarooni." James Robison, who is a preacher, will send you a basket made by an orphan in exchange for a contribution: the orphans "normally work twelve hours a day. Now they're working sixteen hours a day, day and night." Nigeria's minimum wage has been $15.90 a month since 1981. The Franklin Speaking Language Master, offered on QVC, knows 487,000 synonyms—"If it was to just continuously speak all its words, it would take twenty-one hours." Kitchenmate allows you to make both strawberry daiquiris and "mayonnaise in a jar with a room-temperature egg in twenty seconds." In the movie *Starman,* an alien is revivifying a deer that had been strapped to a hunter's pickup. Dr. J is addressing the Converse kids' basketball clinic, offering helpful advice on how to deal with the media after the game and what to do when celebrities want to visit the locker room. Davey and Goliath, and of course a poor boy they're being nice to, are trying to collect enough bottles so they'll be able to afford the Saturday matinee of *Boy in Space.* Oprah Winfrey did have a baby when she was fourteen, but it was premature and quickly died. An "end-time prophet" on one of the religious stations is building a Denver headquarters—"Denver is perfectly located between Frankfurt, Germany, and Tokyo, Japan, so I understand why God is giving us this building," she says. A new program, *You and Me, Kids,* shows parents how to have fun with their kids—"Let's pretend you're a spider and now let's pretend that your mom is the stuff you make webs from." Robert Reed—Mike Brady—has grown a mustache and also found a "breakthrough technology" to "reprogram you for success." He points out that only 12 percent of your mind is conscious, and Art Fleming agrees—after listening to some tapes they know about, a boy "has started to wear colorful clothes, which he never would wear before." The financial markets, according to ABC, "are waiting for the new unemployment figures. It all has to do with how those new unemployment numbers show up. Too many new jobs could tip the Fed into raising interest rates." Car sales rose a cheerful 4.1 percent in the first ten days of April, but business travel to St. Louis will be delayed one hour and five minutes due to fog. The traffic copter notes that "someone on the shoulder of Muddy Branch Road is changing his tire." On Country Music Television a singer laments that "pretty girls are a dime a dozen, and I only got a nickel to my name." Some oldsters are sitting on a sofa, being interviewed for a plumbing ad—"When I was a girl, water didn't come to us, we went to water. We had a well, and we pumped her. Colors? I don't remember any. Styles? We had styles of dresses, not faucets." On *Now You're Cooking*, a lady is making pigs-in-a-blanket with a Super Snacker. "We have a pact in our house—the first one up plugs in the Super Snacker."

And on the pond, the duck is just swimming back and forth, his chest pushing out a wedge of ripples that catch the early rays of the sun.

AFTERWORD

When I finished writing this book, I felt free to give up television without having to think of myself as an intellectual snob. I'd given it its due, and felt that I had learned much of what it had to tell me. Since then, I've seen just enough, in hotel rooms and on airplane seatbacks, to feel confident that the points here are more valid now than when I originally wrote them. But I'm pleased by the publication of a new edition, because it allows me to underline what in retrospect I decided was the most important lesson of this book.

Much came across the cable in my endless day, of course—the insights, such as they are, make up the content of my study. But the most important message is one that really occurred to me somewhat later: If you filter out all the messages that television sends us, if you boil the sap down into syrup—there's an underlying premise: *You are the most important thing on earth*. You, sitting there on the sofa, clutching the remote, are the heaviest object in the known universe. Around you must everything orbit. This Bud's for *you.*

That seems like a very normal idea to us. We've been raised as good consumers, and consumers, above all, put their own interests first. But in fact it's clearly a strange idea for human beings. At other points in history, people have clearly made different things central to their identity: community or tribe, God, nature. And having such identity close to your core mattered, precisely because it allowed you to set limits, to set different priorities.

I'm above all an environmentalist. I wrote this book in the first place to help myself understand why we were so unable as a society to change our lives in even small ways to help combat global warming. And, to an environmentalist, limits are important. If we understood our identity to be linked in some real way to the natural world around us, for instance, we'd be both more worried and more ashamed than we are about filling the atmosphere with carbon dioxide and destabilizing the earth's climate. If we understand ourselves to be, in some deep sense, members of a community, we wouldn't allow our neighbors to live the kinds of blighted lives revealed to us in the aftermath of Hurricane Katrina. We'd spend the tax money to build vital cities, as the Europeans have done—cities that, say, make use of public transit, allowing the average Frenchman or Italian to use half the energy of the average American. This in turn makes the next hurricane less likely. And so on. Europeans still have the sense that they are in part creatures of a community, a sentiment that has been banished from the American mindset.

We, however, have been in the business of eliminating limits in the name of individual freedom. Some of those taboos and limits needed to go—the erosion of race and gender bias is, for instance, all to the good—but the larger process has gone very far indeed in our society. We have become, in the TV decades, not just individualistic but hyperindividualistic, a nation of people who sit alone in big cars, who build ever bigger and more isolated houses (even as the size of our families shrinks). And television has been a clear enabler of this trend, as well as its beneficiary. Robert Putnam, in his recent classic *Bowling Alone*, argues that the spread of TV, more than any other force, devastated civic involvement for Americans—why go out to a meeting when there's always the easy alternative of Jon Stewart? Additionally, in her book *The Overspent American*, Juliet Schor demonstrates that the biggest reason behind our consumption boom is that we've stopped comparing ourselves to our neighbors and started comparing ourselves to the people we see on TV.

If you think I'm overstating the case for individualism, consider the mother of all "reality" television shows, *Survivor*, which spawned a genre that now fills screens at every hour. Here's the premise: You are stranded on a desert island, and the way to win is to force everyone else to leave. And if you can manage that, you'll get a lot of money. In healthier cultures, the response to being stranded is to work together—but "together" is a tough sell for Americans. We don't want to ride the bus with other people—we'd rather drive alone. We take great pleasure in watching Donald Trump fire people.

Since I wrote this book, of course, a new screen has come to share dominance in many of our lives. It's tough to try to figure out how the Internet fits into this picture. It clearly shares some features with television—there's the same physical unreality, the same ability to suck up infinite hours of our time, and the same isolation from other people and the natural world. But it is clearly different as well. Most important, it works both ways—you send and receive. Thus it allows one to form communities, the very thing that TV has undermined so effectively.

These communities have their flaws—they can be essentially anonymous, some of the relations fraudulent. More to the point, they don't resemble human communities in that they assemble themselves by shared interest instead of shared geography. You can spend a lifetime on the Web with people Just Like You, which is a kind of solipsism not that far removed from the hyperindividualism I've been describing.

And yet people do use this technology in other exciting ways. I remember watching Howard Dean's campaign for president develop on the Web in 2003, for instance. Whatever one thinks of his policies, he clearly managed to create a community of people enthused enough to give tens of millions of dollars to his campaign. And his supporters were able to use the Web to arrange thousands of in-the-flesh meetings, the famous Meet-Ups in church basements and high school gyms across the country.

I don't know how the Internet will play out in this regard. (Though I haven't unplugged my connection yet.) I do think that the key question will be whether it breeds deeper community and connection, or deeper isolation and individualism. If this new screen can wean us back in the direction of reality (as opposed to "reality") it will have done a useful service.

INDEX

ABOUT THE AUTHOR

BILL MCKIBBEN has written about the natural world for publications ranging from *The New York Review of Books* and *The New York Times* to *Outside* and *Rolling Stone*. A former staff writer for *The New Yorker*, he has written many books on the media and the environment. He lives with his wife and daughter in the Adirondack mountains of New York State.

ABOUT THE TYPE

The text of this book was set in Janson, a misnamed typeface designed in about 1690 by Nicholas Kis, a Hungarian in Amsterdam. In 1919 the matrices became the property of the Stempel Foundry in Frankfurt. It is an old-style book face of excellent clarity and sharpness. Janson serifs are concave and splayed; the contrast between thick and thin strokes is marked.